Teaching Children to Write Great Poetry

Teaching Children to Write Great Poetry

A practical guide for getting kids' creative juices flowing

HAZEL BENNETT

Edgware Books   London

© Hazel Bennett

Front cover © Sharon Johnston

TEACHING CHILDREN TO WRITE GREAT POETRY

All the pupils' support sheets can be downloaded free from the author's website www.hazelbennett.co.uk/ebooks.html

FOREWORD

WHAT MAKES A POEM?

My various dictionaries describe a poem as an artistic composition in verse, in elevated language, especially of an impassioned or imaginative kind, containing other elements like metre, rhythm, rhyme, powerful imagery to depict series of events or descriptions.

There are many types of poem. Many children (and some teachers) find writing poetry daunting as it can be complicated, and frustrating when the metre, rhythm and rhyme just will not combine to express what you want to say in an original or attention grabbing way.

The aim of this book is to give teachers ideas to present in the classroom to make the art of writing poetry accessible and enjoyable for children.

WHY WRITE POETRY?

Apart from fulfilling the objectives of the National Curriculum, children derive great satisfaction from writing poetry. Also, the practice in thinking out interesting expressions, and descriptive vocabulary enhances the quality of their creative writing.

As well as that, it is great fun and children gain a lot of pleasure and the sense of achievement which writing poetry gives them.

TOOLS TO WRITE POEMS

1   ALLITERATION

Alliteration occurs when a few words, which are close together, start with the same letter or sound. Using alliteration makes children think up engaging vocabulary.

It is an ear-catching technique used at all levels in both poetry and prose. The author Francesca Simon uses it successfully in her Horrid Henry books with Moody Margaret and Perfect Peter. The nursery rhyme's opening line, 'Sing a song of sixpence,' grabs children's attention. Experts, like the poet Gerard Manley Hopkins, used alternate alliteration as in his poem, 'When kingfishers catch fire, dragon flies draw flame.'

The Anglo-Saxons, who were great story tellers and poets, considered alliteration to be more important than rhyming in poetry.

Lesson 1

Objective: to write an interesting alliterative class poem.

Warm-up

Read alliterative poems which are suitable for your pupils' age-group. *Dr Seuss* books contain examples of alliterative poems. Younger Key Stage 2 children love the traditional alliterative tongue-twister rhyme.

> Peter Piper picked a peck of pickled peppers.
> A peck of pickled peppers Peter Piper picked.
> If Peter Piper picked a peck of pickled peppers,
> How many pickled peppers did Peter Piper pick?
>
> Sheila sells seashells on the sea shore
> Where's the shells that Sheila sells on the sea shore?

Point out the alliterative first lines which grab the attention of small children in various nursery rhymes.

> Sing a song of sixpence,

Wee Willie Winkie
Baa-baa black sheep,
Bye, Baby Bunting
Jack and Jill

For older children, you can google lots of suitable poems by typing 'alliterative poems for children' into the search bar. Unfortunately I cannot print them here because of copyright.

Read these and ask pupils to comment on the effect of the alliteration in the first two lines. They are reproduced here by kind permission of Christopher Matthew.

Hebblethwaite and Hopwood
Fothergill and Fenn
And Bob Stanford-Dingley
Are five grown men
And all of them are ogling our barmaid, Jen.   Christopher Matthew

Read these to older Key Stage 2 and lower Key Stage 3. Gerard Manley Hopkins' powerful *Pied Beauty* never fails to impress me.

Glory be to God for dappled things-
For skies of couple-colour as a brinded cow;
For rose-moles all in stipple upon trout that swim;
Fresh-firecoal chestnut-falls; finches wings;
Landscape, plotted and pierced – fold, fallow and plough;
And all trades their gear and tackle and trim.

And this extract also by Gerard Manley Hopkins. Point out how using words like 'breath' and 'bread' in the same phrase make it stronger.

Thou mastering me
God! Giver of breath and bread;
World's strand, sway of the sea:
Lord of living and dead;
Thou hast bound bones and veins in me, fastened me flesh.

Ask pupils to comment on the effect of the alliteration.

Main part

Start by asking children for a list of things they like. Write them by the side of the board ready to make notes. It might look like this:

Football

Netball

Music

Wii

Play-station

Parties

Seaside

Holidays

Mangoes

Grandma

Sleepovers

Harry Potter

Now ask then to think up adjectives or phrases for each containing an alliteration and write them alongside their noun. Like this:-

Football	fabulous fun, full of fight, fierce attacking, fast
Netball	neat goals, never boring
Music	makes me happy, moods,
Wii	weekends of fun, working hard to win
Sunny weather	super, sweaty, swimming, warm
Parties	playing games,
Seaside	smooth sea, seagulls swooping, shrimps swimming in pools, spading sand,
Holidays	happy days, having fun,
Mangoes	make my mouth water, melt on my tongue,
Grandma	gives me a good feeling,
Harry Potter	high adventure, playing quidditch
Sweets	sticky, sickly sweet, squelchy
Science fiction	exciting stories,
Chocolate	chunks, crunch.

Teaching points to emphasize

* Alliteration makes a description interesting and attractive.

- It is the sound which causes the alliteration. It may be made by a different letter as in 'exciting stories' (underlined).

- Not all poetry has to rhyme. Sometimes the language creates satisfying pictures and feelings which are best left as they are.

Ask children to convert their suggested words into phrases containing alliteration. They might suggest something like this.

> Warm sunny weather to go to the lido to swim with my friends
>
> Science fiction makes exciting films
>
> Chunks of chocolate
>
> Mangoes melting in my mouth
>
> Fast games of football
>
> Sticky chewy sweets
>
> Playing with my spades on the sand
>
> Playing with my Wii at the week-end

Now tell them to think of rhythm. Recite a line clapping the rhythm, and counting the number of beats or stressed syllables in each line. Suggest turning the lines into poetry by giving an even rhythm. Using four long or stressed syllables (feet) in each line works well. Take each line in turn, and ask pupils to lengthen or shorten each line to make four stressed syllables. Clap the beat of the lines so that the children can hear the rhythm.

Example,

> Warm, sunny weather to go to the lido to swim with friends,

can be cut down to

> Warm sunny weather to swim with my friends.
>
> Chunks of chocolate

can be lengthened to

> Chunks of chocolate that I love to crunch.

Put them together to read the poem so far. It might be on this pattern.

Things I love

Warm, sunny weather to swim with friends,

Exciting science fiction in films,

Granddad, who gives me a good time and great fun,

Square chunks of chocolate that I love to crunch,

Mangoes, so scrumptious they melt in my mouth,

Fast games of football and fighting to win,

Sweets all sticky and chewy and delicious,

Spading the sand by a clear smooth sea,

Week-ends of fun on my Wii and play station,

Now give pupils ten minutes to work in pairs to write down some more things they love, in alliterative phrases of four beats.

Ask for a suggestion from each pair and write as many as you can on the board.

Differentiation

Pair children who need support with those who are better writers, because often the former can produce interesting ideas for the other to scribe.

Plenary

Class reads their completed alliterative poem together. Challenge them to suggest an effective final rhyming couplet to sum it all up. For example,

Granny giving gifts generously,

These are the things that are special to me.

Tell pupils that in the next lesson, they will write their own poems about things which they hate, so that they can be thinking of things to include and make a list.

Lesson 2

Objective: to write their own alliterative poems on the topic of 'Things I hate'.

Warm-up

Recap on the previous lesson. Remind children of the benefit of alliteration to make descriptions ear-catching and attractive.

Children write their own list of things they hate.

Main part

Remind pupils of the procedure of lesson 1 and tell them to use the same procedure on the theme of things I hate. Working, in pairs, they make a list of things they hate and write them in a column, and add phrases and adjectives with alliteration. Their list might look like this.

Homework	horrible, horrid, gives me a headache
Worms	worst feeling, wish they weren't here, wiggle
Snakes	slithery, slimy, squirm, scaly
Rats	revolting, roving over the grass
Bullies	bad, breaking up everyone's games, brutal
Angry adults	asking the impossible, always
Handwriting	hurting my hand,
Rain	rattling on the roof tops, running down my ankles, ruining our games
Spiders	squirm, shiver, make me scream

Then they make up a list of phrases using these alliterations.

Teaching points to remind the children

• It does not matter if they do not rhyme. Interesting words are more important.

• Use four long syllables or beats in a line to get an even rhythm.

• It is the sound which matters: alliteration can still be made by different letters.

Ask for a suggestion from each pair and write as many as you can on the board.

Things I hate

Bullies who break up our games and bring trouble,

Spiders that squiggle and make me squirm,

Slithering snakes all slimy and scaly,

Rain that rattles on roofs and ruins play,

Revolting rats that rove in the alleyway,

Adults always angry with kids

Horrible homework, when I'd rather play

Handwriting practice that hurts my hand.

Differentiation

Either, pair up less able writers with more competent writers, or the teacher works with the children, who need learning support in a small group, to help them to write a group poem.

Plenary

Some children read their alliterative lines aloud. As in Lesson 1, challenge the children to add an effective rhyming couplet to sum up the whole list. For example,

Worms wiggling round withering weeds.

These are the things that no child needs.

Extension work for a future lesson

Look at whatever period you are studying in history, or country in geography. Write a description of its people, their homes, their lifestyle and occupations using some alliterative phrases. (Remind children that alliterative phrases in prose are more effective if used occasionally because sometimes children spoil their work by trying to use them in every sentence.)

2   METAPHORS

A metaphor is a phrase, which does not apply literally, to illustrate something. It should not be confused with a simile which says that something is like another thing. Metaphors create powerful images and improve the quality of both poetry and prose.

Work with metaphors is suitable for older Key Stage 2 and younger KS3 children.

A list of common metaphors

Bull in a china shop	clumsy person
Bear with a sore head	grumpy, irritable person
Pillar of the community	person who works hard for the people around them
Flea in the ear	short, sharp reprimand
Sword of Damocles	a worry which hangs over you
Pour oil on troubled water	stop people arguing
Spanner in the works	person or thing stopping things from working properly
Pain in the neck	annoying person or thing
Wake-up call	reminder of danger
Red herring	misleading clue, something which takes attention away from the important issue
Food for thought	something to provoke a lot of thinking
Cut off your nose to spite your face	create problems for yourself
Walk on water	achieve incredibly highly
Between the devil and the deep blue sea	caught in a dilemma between two difficulties
Leave no stone unturned	make a thorough investigation

Frog in the throat	congestion in your tubes, causing discomfort, coughing
A sprat to catch a mackerel	a small risk to gain something much greater
To buy a pig in a poke	to buy something without seeing it properly to see if it is useful
Cast pearls before swine	give something valuable to someone who does not appreciate it.

Lesson 1

Objective: to understand metaphors and how to use them effectively.

Warm-up

Introduce the term 'metaphor' and explain its meaning. Give a few examples from the list above. Present a few more and ask children to work out their meanings. Check that the children understand the following points.

- Metaphors label a person or object with a phrase which is not to be taken literally.

- Metaphors are not similes. They do not say that one thing is like another.

- Metaphors are a great aide to poets and writers because of the power which they give to descriptions. They conjure up a lot of images with a few words.

Read the examples below to see how effectively John Keats, 1819, used the metaphors of the lily and the rose in this verse from 'La belle dame sans merci.'

> I see a lily on thy brow,
> With anguish moist and fever-dew,
> And on thy cheek a fading rose
> Fast withereth too.

In the song, 'I'll take you home again, Kathleen', the songwriter Thomas Westendorf, 1875, used it similarly.

> The roses all have left your cheeks.
> I've watched them fade away and die.

Invite them to describe what the words 'lily' and 'roses' suggest in these examples.

Read this verse from D. H. Lawrence's poem, *Bat*.

Look up, and you can see things flying,
Between the day and the night.
Swallows with spools of dark thread, sewing the shadows together.

Ask pupils to describe the picture created in their mind with the metaphor of swallows sewing the shadows together with dark thread.

Teaching points

* Metaphors use a few words to describe something that might take up to two or three sentences of prose.

* The fewer words you use, the more powerful it is.

Ask pupils to pick out the metaphors in this verse from Alfred Noyes' poem, 'The Highwayman'.

The wind was a torrent of darkness among the gusty trees,
The moon was a ghostly galleon tossed upon cloudy seas,
The road was a ribbon of moonlight over the purple moor
And the highwayman came riding, riding, riding
The highwayman came riding up to the old inn door.

Reproduced here by kind permission of the Society of Authors on behalf of the Alfred Noyes Estate.

Ask how do the metaphors in the first three lines add power to the wind, moon and road and conjure up images in the readers' imaginations.

Main part

Point out that sometimes people use unsuitable metaphors destroying their effect and sometimes people mix metaphors and use them inappropriately, as in -

'The only thing this government will listen to is muscle. This tower of strength will forge ahead.'

Ask them to explain why the first sentence sounds silly and how the second metaphor spoils the effect of the first.

Emphasize that:

* metaphors are more effective if used occasionally, not in every sentence;

- there should never be more than one applied to any one person and thing;

- metaphors enhance the quality of description in prose as well as poetry;

- as with similes, the standard metaphors have lost their ability to surprise, so when writers use metaphors they usually think up their own.

Start with the examples of a bull in a china shop for a clumsy person, and a bear with a sore head for a grumpy, irritable person. Think up a list of types of people for which you could invent metaphors. Write them down them left hand side of the board as in the example below.

Aggressive person

Shy person

Happy person

Sad person

Forgetful person

Angry person

Kind person

Clever person

Bossy person

Generous person

Mean person

Agile person

Dishonest person

Now ask the children to suggest orally metaphors for each.

Examples

aggressive person	a hungry tiger
generous person	an ever open purse
angry person	a ball of fire

Plenary

Children choose a metaphor each and suggest sentences using it in an interesting way, like in this example.

Our teacher was a ball of fire when our football went through the window of his new car.

Lesson 2

Objective: to use metaphors to write poems or imaginative prose

Warm-up

Recap on the previous lesson to remind children of the meaning of 'metaphor'.

Put the children into pairs and give each pair a copy of the next page for them to join the metaphors and their meanings.

METAPHORS

Join the metaphors with their meanings. Use a different colour for each one.

A bear with a sore head	old-age
A rose among thorns	reaching the point of exhaustion
A running sore	grumpy person
The apple of my eye	miserable person
Between a rock and a hard place	constant annoyance
Thorn in the side	person or thing that spoils something good
A breath of fresh air	someone greatly loved
She's flying	kindly person among less lovable people
On your last legs	something or someone annoying
Fly in the ointment	begin to cope with a lot of problems
A wet blanket	she's achieving a string of successes
Get your neck above the water	caught between two problems
The evening of your life	a pleasant cheerful happy person
raining cats and dogs	great lack of care
pull your socks up	great kindness
heart of stone	courage
heart of a lion	raining very heavily
heart of gold	work harder
icing on the cake	something extra to make it special

Main part

Suggest a scenario to the class, e.g. a storm. There are lots of pictures on www.picsearch.co.uk to use as a stimulus, either in hard copy or on an IWB.

Ask what things are active in the picture – wind, thunder, lightning, sea, birds, ship, people. Now ask for metaphors for each. You might get ideas like these.

Wind	the howl of angry wolves
Thunder and lightning	God's anger, bombs exploding in the sky
Sea	an angry torrent
Birds	pieces of black paper tossed in the sky
Ship	a toy rocked on the waves
People	powerless stick insects

Repeat this with another picture, for example, a rain forest.

Tropical birds	splashes of vivid colours
Vegetation	giant green monsters reaching for prey
Monkeys	playful jack-in-the-boxes exploring the trees
Insects	deadly swarms of punctuation marks

Or a funfair

Rollercoaster	giant caterpillar dashing at breakneck speed
Octopus ride	green monster twirling its prey
Spanish waltzer	dizzy cars
Big dipper	a wheel with spokes of giant soup ladles
Gondolas	floating beds

Children, in mixed groups of three or four, choose a picture and write a poem or descriptive prose using metaphors to describe the different parts. If necessary, make sure that that each group has an able writer to scribe for the group.

Teaching points

- Imagine that the reader cannot see the picture so you want to them to see it in their mind's eye when reading their description.

- Put in an interesting opening sentence.

- Only write one metaphor for each item.

- Metaphors can be over-used so it is fine to have some sentences without them.

- It does not have to rhyme. If there is imaginative language which creates pictures in the mind, it is better not to spoil it by putting in something inappropriate to make it rhyme.

- Emphasise that this is descriptive work. There is no need for a plot with characters.

- Put in an interesting final sentence.

Spend some time listening in to each group to ensure that the less able writers have their chance to contribute.

Plenary

Read their descriptions to the class. Ask children to describe the images, which the metaphors create in their minds. Remind children that metaphors are a useful tool for both poetry and prose.

3 ONOMATOPOEIA

Onomatopoeia is a word or set of words which are formed to imitate the sound for which they stand.

Children love the word 'onomatopoeia'. They love to repeat it, possibly because it has something sophisticated in a Mary Poppins sort of way.

To prepare for this lesson, make flashcards of rhyming words for the children to match up in rhyming pairs. Use the list suggested in the main part of the lesson.

Lesson 1

Objective: to examine onomatopoeia and use it in writing poems

Warm up

Have ready a variety of percussion and wind instruments and/or objects which will make a sound – bottle with some water in it to tap, tins, wrapping paper, coins.

Write 'onomatopoeia' on the board and ask children if they know its meaning. Explain that it is a word which imitates a sound and give examples – bang, thud, rat-a-tat, crash, splash. Get children, in turn, to use the objects and instruments to make sounds. Ask for suggestions of words of onomatopoeia for each sound.

Main part

Read this extract from Robert Browning's 'Pied Piper' and ask the children to point out the sound words and ask them to comment on the effect they have on the poems.

> In to the street the piper **stept**
> Smiling first a little smile,

As if he knew what magic slept
In his quiet pipe the while;
Then, like a musical adept,
To blow the pipe his lips he wrinkled,
And green and blue his sharp eyes twinkled,
Like a candle-flamed where salt was sprinkled;
And ere three shrill notes the pipe **uttered**,
You heard as if a army **muttered**;
The **muttering** grew to a **grumbling**;
And the **grumbling** grew to mighty **rumbling**;
And out of the house the rats came **tumbling**.   Robert Browning

And this rhyme

In the **cuckoo** clock, the **cuckoo** sang
And the kettle **whistled** on the stove.
The back-door **slammed** and the doorbell **dinged**
And the telephone **rang-rang-rang.**   H. A. Bennett

And this

I heard the ripple **washing** on the reeds
And the wild water **lapping** on the crag.
                    from *Morte d'Arthur*   Alfred Lord Tennyson

Class brainstorms lots of words of onomatopoeia. The words below might help to
supplement your list.

woof

clap, rap, slap, snap

click, tick

boom, zoom

brrrm-brrrm

rat-a-tat

fizz, whizz

clang, bang

smash, crash, splash, slash

thump bump

honk

ding-dong, ping-pong

toot, hoot

growl, howl

pop, clippety-clop, plop, slop, flop

munch, crunch

cuckoo, boo

wow, meow

kerplunk, clunk

racket

whoosh shoosh

buzz

whirr, purr

squeak, shriek

mumble, rumble

hush, flush, gush

tinkle, clinkle

chime

toll

moan, groan

crackle, cackle

rustle, bustle

hiss, kiss

yakkety-yak

slurp, burp

gurgle,

rip, zip

munch, crunch

whisper

tick tock.

clink, tink

sizzle, fizzle

rattle, prattle, brattle

clatter, shatter

thwack, clicketty-clack, whack, smack, crack

thud

ping, ring

Main part

On the carpet set out the flashcards of sound words randomly with the children sitting in a circle round them. Divide the class circle into two semicircles to make two teams.

Choose one child from each team to find as many rhyming pairs as they can in fifteen seconds. Then another child from each team for fifteen seconds until everyone has had a try. The team with the most rhyming pairs wins.

Pick a 'noisy' title like a band. Talk about instruments in a band and ask children to suggest onomatopoeia words to describe their sound. Write them in a column on the board and ask the children to suggest rhyming words, like this.

bang, clang, sang, rang

toot, hoot, flute

tinkle, clinkle

bong, ding-dong, song

chime, rhyme, time

rap, slap, clap, tap

In pairs, they begin writing descriptions or a poem about a band, using the rhyming onomatopoeia words to write their poem.

Differentiation

The next page will help some children to get started. The following page is for the lower ability pupils, to give them some prompts for the starting and the finishing lines. The list of instruments at the end is to jog their memory of instruments to use.

Plenary

The children read a few of their poems to the class. Set the task of composing introductory lines for the beginning, and thinking up effective ending lines to sum up their thoughts about the band.

Use this to help you write your poem. At the end of each line, you can cross out the sound word which you do not want, or change them. Add some lines of your own.

The Band

_____

_____ bong

_____ song

_____ hoot   toot

_____ flute

_____ tinkle

_____ clinkle

_____chime time

_____ rhyme

_____ bang clang

_____ rang sang

_____ rap clap

_____tap slap

_____

_____

Use this to help you start your poem. You can change the sound words at the end of the line if you wish, and add some of your own.

The Band

The children _____ meet

The brass band _____ street

_____ song bong

_____ding-dong

_____ hoot   toot

_____ flute

_____ tinkle

_____ clinkle

_____ chime time

_____ rhyme

_____ bang clang

_____ rang sang

_____ rap clap

_____tap slap

They _____and sang along

And _____all day long.

These musical instruments might help you to think up lines.

trumpet, triangle, drum, clarinet, trombone, chime bar, chime bell, piccolo, cornet, saxophone, flute, cymbals, accordion

Lesson 2

Objective: to write poems using onomatopoeia

Warm up

This activity can be carried out with the title *The Farm*. Show children pictures of farm scenes. Class brainstorm animals they might see on a farm. Write their names on the left-hand side of the board and add the sound words to go with each one. Include a few wild animals and birds as well as domesticated animals to make it easier to find rhymes. Your list might look like this.

cow	moo
bull	roar, bellow
dog	bark, growl, woof
cat	meow, purr, yowl
pig, boar, sow	snore, snort, grunt, squeal
horse	clippetty-clop, whimper, neigh
sheep	bleat, ma-a-a-a
turkey	gobble
goose	cackle
hen	cluck,
duck	quack
cockerel	cock-a-doodle-doo
hedgehog	snuffle, shuffle
mouse	squeak
rat	squeak, scrape
fox	howl, screech
woodpecker	tap
owl	hoot, flap,
cuckoo	cuckoo,

Tell the children to put their suggestions into rhyming pairs and groups. Write them on the board as the children suggest them. Add the names of animals and other suitable farm words like 'hoof 'and 'haystack' into the appropriate rhyming group. Your notes may look like this.

cow, meow, sow

howl, fowl, growl, owl, growl,

cuckoo, moo, cock-a-doddle-doo, too-whit-too-woo

hoot, dove-coot,

flap, tap

mouse, farmhouse

snuffle, shuffle

cluck, duck

roar, snore, boar

bellow, fellow

bark, lark

woof, hoof

purr, stir

snort

grunt

clippetty-clop

whimper

neigh, lay

bleat, eat

ma-a-a-a

gobble, hobble

cackle

cluck, duck

quack, haystack

lazing, grazing

squeal, wheel

Now use your bank of rhyming words to build up some verses about a day on the farm.

Teaching points

*   They do not have to use rhyming couplets. They can have alternate line rhyming.

31

- The rhymes do not need to come at the end of the line. They can have them scattered along the lines.
- They can write poems with lots of onomatopoeia and interesting words but no rhyming.
- Remember to use their other poetry skills – alliteration, similes, metaphors

Differentiation

After the practice in lesson 1, most should be able to work without a frame, but the writing frame on the next page makes the task easier for the children who need support. The hardest part is getting started, so give this as a suggestion to anyone who needs it to get going.

There's a city farm near my school.

We saw lots of animals. It was really cool.

Plenary

Some children read their poems out to the class. Challenge them to suggest interesting final lines to sum up their feeling about their day at the farm.

A day at the farm

There's a city farm near my school.
We saw lots of animals. It was really cool.
We saw naughty young puppies all playful and yapping
Scaring the chickens and sending them flapping.

And in the field _____ lazing.

Cows _____ grazing.

The bull _____ bellow.

Don't _____ fellow.

Creeping _____ farmhouse.

I _____ mouse.

Pigs _____ grunting

Little piglets _____ pushing and shunting.

Squealing _____ gruffy old boar.

He _____snore.

In the fields _____ haystacks.

Ducks _____ quacks.

Sheep _____ bleating.

_____ eating.

_____

I'd love to go another day

And hear _____

4   RHYMING

Although rhyming words are associated with poetry they are not absolutely essential in every type of poem. Many poems stand well without them, but nonetheless, a poem with rhymes impresses.

Children often try to use inappropriate words for the sake of making their poem rhyme, and in doing so, they spoil it. It is important to emphasize that sense is more important than rhyme.

Lesson Plan

Objective: to recognise rhyming words and write rhyming couplets.

Warm up

Make sure that the children understand the term 'rhyming' words.

Play snap with rhyming words. Show children the following words in pairs, either on flashcards or type them onto an IWB, in advance and reveal them in pairs. If the words rhyme, the children say 'Snap' or it is more orderly if you ask for a show of hands to the questions 'Do these rhyme?' then, 'Not rhyme?'

hear	bear
soap	hope
sail	tale
worry	sorry
carry	marry
catch	watch
show	now

shine   mine

piece   release

perhaps   collapse

hurry   worry

Ask the children what they notice about rhyming words. Check that they realise that words may look like rhyming words, but they are not, and vice versa. Emphasise that it the sound which counts not the letter string.

Rhyming game

On an IWB, prepare a page with these words written individually so that they can be moved around.

share   green   seaside   sight   fairy   gave   rain   wonder

scary   hair   tried   mane   thunder   bite   bean   wave

lean   declare   spied   polite   under   lane   rave   hairy

scene   height   shave   blunder   flare   outside   wary   plane

Give the children a few minutes to study them and then ask them to pick out rhyming words to move into groups. It is more efficient if the children suggest the rhyming pairs and the teacher moves them with a mouse. Letting the pupils do it manually, in turn, slows the lesson down and the children become bored.

If you have no IWB, this can be done by putting cards with one word on each onto the carpet, with children sitting in a circle around them. Ask children, in turn, to find rhyming words. You can make this fun by using a stop watch, or second timer on a clock, to time children to see who can find most pairs in a set time, like ten seconds. Let the more able pupils start because it is easier to find pairs when there are fewer cards to read.

When all the cards have been lifted, children hold up the words in sets – there are 4 for each sound - and read them to reinforce the point that they do not have to have the same letter strings to rhyme, and sometimes the same letter strings produce a different sound.

Main part

Show children how to use a rhyming dictionary. Emphasize that the same final sound can be shown in different ways: -oo, -ew, -ue, u-e etc.

Give pupils these starting lines, and ask them to choose one or more to write a continuation line with the last words rhyming. They can work in pairs or individually.

> A dinosaur went out one day
>
> The snow was floating softly down
>
> The birds were nesting in the trees
>
> The footballer was running fast
>
> The dancers glided across the floor
>
> The pirate ship sailed out to sea
>
> I lost my library book last week
>
> Last week-end, I was bored with nothing to do
>
> Last night, we were playing in the park

Differentiation:

Children who need support can use the sheet at the end of the chapter.

Plenary

Children read their rhyming couplets to the rest of the class. Challenge them to add more rhyming lines to build it up onto a short verse.

RHYMING

Write a second line to rhyme with the first. You can use the words at the end.

A dinosaur went out one day

_____

play, grey, way,

stay, hay, lay,

The snow was floating softly down

_____

brown, frown,

town, drown

The birds were nesting in the trees

_____

breeze, freeze

please, squeeze ease

The footballer was running fast

_____

passed, last,

past, blast

The dancers glided across the floor

_____

more, door,

sore, bore

The pirate ship sailed up to the land

_____

sand, grand,

planned, stand strand

Last week-end, I was bored with nothing to do

_____

zoo, drew, glue, Until I

threw, new

5 SIMILES

A simile is an expression which compares two things because of some strong resemblance. There are many in the English language. They enhance descriptions in both poetry and prose.

Lesson 1

Objective: to understand similes and their use in improving poetry and prose

Warm up

Explain the meaning of simile and tell children that they usually contain the words 'like' and 'as' for comparison. Ask children for common examples. There are many.

Add these common examples to add to their list, if necessary.

as green as grass	as blue as the sky	as happy as a lark
as white as snow	as sweet as apple pie	as proud as a peacock
as yellow as corn	as warm as toast	as good as gold
as red as blood	as cold as ice	as bright as a button
as black as tar	as quiet as a mouse	as long as a wet week

Read Christina Rossetti's poem and ask the children to identify the similes and comment on their effect.

Flint
An emerald is as green as grass,
A ruby red as blood;
A sapphire shines as blue as heaven;
A flint lies in the mud.

A diamond is a brilliant stone,
To catch the world's desire;
An opal holds a fiery spark;
But a flint holds fire.

Read these examples and ask children to identify the similes used.

O My Luve's like a red, red rose,
That's newly sprung in June;
O My Luve's like the melodie
That's sweetly played in tune.   Robert Burns

I wandered lonely as a cloud
That floats on high o'er vales and hills   William Wordsworth

Bats!
Hanging upside down like rows of disgusting old rags
And grinning in their sleep   D.H.Lawrence

Ask them to describe the picture which each simile creates in their minds. Explain that similes are great for descriptions but the common similes, like the ones already mentioned at the beginning, are now so old that they have lost their ability to surprise and entertain. Writers call them 'old clichés' and do not use them. Explain that in order to make their work interesting and exciting it is better to think up their own.

Main lesson

Take the examples already used to make up new similes, orally. They can work in small groups, pairs or singly.

as green as _____

as white as a _____

as yellow as _____

as red as _____

as black as _____

as blue as a _____

as sweet as _____

as warm as _____

as cold as _____

as quiet as _____

as happy as _____

as proud as _____

as good as _____

as bright as _____

as long as _____

Ask the children to work in pairs or singly to think of any creature which they like. Make the range as wide as possible – living, extinct, mammal, fish, bird, insect, real or mythical and tell them to write down as many similes as they can to describe that creature's characteristics. Advise them to choose a creature which has lots of characteristics about which to write.

Remind them that it is more effective to think up their own original simile than use the common one. Use this example to get them started.

A bull

horns like cucumbers

as fierce as a crocodile if you annoy it

hooves as hard as stone

Plenary

Choose children to read their similes out to the class without the title, for the others to guess the name of the creature. Challenge the class to add one more simile to each list read out. Tell them that they will use them in the next lesson to write a poem.

Lesson 2

(This is a challenging activity so classes might need a further session to finish.)

Objective   To write poems about animals using similes

Warm up

Recap on previous lesson. Remind children about similes, their uses and effect.

Ask children to complete these, either giving the traditional simile or one of their own.

as fresh as_____   as young as _____

as old as _____   as bitter as _____

as soft as _____   as hard as _____

as nice as _____   as thick as _____

Main part

Show children how to use a rhyming dictionary to find other words which might rhyme with the word they want to use.

Explain that they are going to use their similes to write a poem about their creature chosen in Lesson 1. Remind them of their list of similes from the previous lesson. Use the example below to model the process. Ask the children to suggest similes for an elephant. Write their suggestions on the board, and add some of these below to the list. Point out that the wider variety they have, the more interesting their poem will be.

Elephant

legs like tree trunks   tail like a ragged skipping rope

body like an water tank   tusks like giant cucumbers

grey as a January sky   strong as Hercules   bellows like thunder

ears like giant leaves   toes like ping pong balls   strong as cast iron

eyes like marbles   trunk like a rubbery gas pipe

crushes twigs like cornflakes

Now tell the children to look for words that might be useful to rhyme or nearly rhyme. Of course they can put in extra words of their own. Advise them that it is not effective to use unsuitable words just to make them rhyme. It is better to have interesting lines, even if they do not rhyme, than awkward ones that do. Add these to the list that they suggest.

trees Hercules   lumbers cucumbers   sky eye   cornflakes takes

tank bank   ping pong along strong   leaves heaves

41

toes hose nose grey way

Work in pairs or singly, the children finish their own lists of similes and add rhyming words to write their own poems about the creatures of their choice. Remind them they can use a rhyming dictionary and the thesaurus.

Differentiation

Children who need support can use the notes on an elephant and the writing frame at the end of the chapter to complete the poem. They can use the words at the end to help make it rhyme or change anything they wish. Encourage them to add lines of their own.

Plenary

Choose different children from lesson 1 to read out their poems so far, without the titles, for children to guess the name of creatures. Challenge the class to add an interesting pair of finishing off lines for the poem.

To link with other subjects

Choose a topic which they are studying in history, RE., geography or science and write a poem about it, using similes.

Elephant

A body like a _____ along.

On legs like _____strong

With toes like _____ ping pong.

He flattens _____cornflakes,

_____stamp he takes.

With ears_____ rain forest trees

_____as strong as Hercules

His _____sky

With _____ eye.

With a trunk _____ nose,

_____ hose.

_____

_____

_____

_____

POEMS WHICH ARE FUN TO WRITE

6   ACROSTIC POEMS

Acrostic poems are poems, of which, usually the first letter of each line spells a word which is the subject of the poem. Occasionally, it is the last letter of the line which spells the word. They are a great starting point for children who believe that they cannot write poetry. Acrostics do not have to rhyme, although it is more impressive of they do, and they can have lines of any length.

Lesson 1

Objective   To recognize acrostic poems and write a class acrostic poem

Warm up

It is easier for the children to see the initial letter word if they can see the poem. IWBs are useful for this. Read these acrostic poems and invite their comments on:-

>   length of line;

>   content;

>   choice of words to describe;

>   senses.

Easy examples.

>   **P**retty feathers
>   **A**ll bright colours
>   **R**adiant shades of
>   **R**ed, yellow and blue,
>   **O**range and green.
>   **T**alks and squawks

>   **C**uddly little pet
>   **A**ttractive soft fur
>   **T**ail of velvet

Hairy little rodent
Always gnawing
Mammal
Silent creeper
Tail almost disappeared
Exercises on a wheel
Races up ladders in his cage

Swirly, spotty fur of black and white
Keeps predators at bay with a smelly spray
Underground burrows are its resting place
Nocturnal creatures who silently hunt
Kills small animals to eat

The Internet can supply thousands of more sophisticated examples like the one below.

Gives you up-to-date information
Or maps of every place and nation
Opens up a world of illustrations
Gives notes on festivals and celebrations
Lets you find websites of organizations
Email addresses of friends and relations   H.A.Bennett

Main part

Write a class acrostic poem. Ask pupils to suggest a creature - real, mythical, extinct, living, of any environment. Write the name of the creature on the board and invite the pupils to brainstorm notes, as in this example.

DOLPHIN

Glides through the air   giant leaps   cone-shaped teeth in rows   graceful dives noiselessly   eats fish   performs tricks in public   smooth skin to glide through the water   warm blooded   mammal   lives in large groups   powerful tail flukes strong muscles   twists and turns in the air   has a blowhole on top to breathe air leaves the blowhole at lightning speed   takes short naps just below the surface of the water   hunts at night

Write the letters down the side of your board and invite children to suggest phrases beginning with the letters. They might suggest something like this.

> **D**ives into the sea
> **O**pens its blowhole to breathe
> **L**eaps through the air
> **P**owerful tail
> **H**elps it to glide along
> **I**n the ocean.
> **N**ight hunter.

Ask for suggestions as to how they can expand each line to make it more interesting. You might improve it like this.

> **D**ives quietly into the sea
> **O**pens its blowhole to breathe
> **L**eaps high, gracefully through the air
> **P**owerful tail fluke
> **H**elps it to glide swiftly along
> **I**n the deep ocean.
> **N**ight hunter of fish.

Discuss how they have improved it with adverbs and more information.

Plenary

Tell the children to choose their own creature to write their own acrostic poem in the next lesson. Children, who need learning support, can be advised to choose creatures with 3 or 4 letters. Encourage the more able to choose longer names like 'rhinoceros'. Emphasize that they should choose something they like and of which they have some knowledge. Give them two minutes´ thinking time. Ask them to tell the class one or two descriptive phrases about their creature for the rest to guess what it is. Tell the pupils that they have until the next lesson to expand their notes with information from books or the Internet.

Lesson 2

Objective   To write their own acrostic poem

Warm up

Recap on meaning of acrostic. Read again the acrostic poem which the class has written collectively on the previous lesson. Remind them of how they improved it.

Main part

Children write down the name of their creatures and make their own notes to help them write their poems. Give children about 15-20 minutes to write their own acrostic poems using their notes.

Differentiation

The hardest part is getting the first word in each line. The sheet at the end of the chapter will make it easier for children who are unable to get started and need more support.

Plenary

Children read their poems to the class and invite others to suggest improvements.

Lesson 3

Objective   To write acrostic poems about children in the class

Warm-up

Recap on the points that make an interesting acrostic poem:–

• plenty of notes with information to give ideas

• adjectives and adverbs

• strong verbs

• senses – sight, sound, smell, feel,

Main part

Ask the children who would like to volunteer to have their name used for a class acrostic poem and write a name on the board. Brainstorm lots of words and phrases to use and write them on your board as in the example below.

Elizabeth

Plays tennis   clever at maths   goes to Greece for her holidays

plays on her playstation loves eating pizza   has a pet puppy called Spot

lives near the park   plays the piano   is good at swimming   hates rats   helps

her mum at home   loves playing computer games

Now write the initial letters at the left-hand side of the page and ask the class to make suggestions to fill in the rest of each line. The first try might look like this.

Example 1

Elizabeth plays on her computer

Lives near the park

Is great on the piano

Zips through maths work

Always wins the swimming races

Bakes cakes with her mum

Eats pizzas

Treats her puppy well

Hates rats

This makes a reasonable first draft. Encourage the children to expand each line into a sentence or a clause with reasonable amount of information. Invite them to make suggestions to extend example 1 into more interesting and detailed lines.

Example 2

Elizabeth plays games on her computer and play station

Lives near the park, and takes her puppy there every day

Is great at playing pop music on the piano

Zips through her maths work and always needs more

Always wins the swimming races in the school gala

Bakes cakes with her mum and shares them with us

Eats pepperoni pizzas and spaghetti bolognese

Travels to Greece for holidays with her family

Hates rats and screams if she sees one.

Now see if you can make any of it rhyme. Choose a simple rhyme scheme. The simplest is to just make the 2nd and 4th lines rhyme and the 6th and 8th lines rhyme. It does not matter if there are any lines left over or if you vary the scheme it to make rhyme.

Example 3

Elizabeth plays games on her computer and play station

Lives near the park, and takes her puppy there to play

Is great at playing pop music on the piano

Zips through her maths work every day

Always wins the swimming races in the school gala

Bakes cakes with her mum and brings them out to share

Eats pepperoni pizzas in our street café

Takes holidays in Greece, she loves it there.

Hates rats, and if she sees one, she quickly runs away.

All of the children write down lots of phrases about themselves. Pupils swap their notes with partners asking the partners to add their suggestions. If you think it necessary, emphasize that negative and insulting comments are not permitted. Each child writes either their own or partner's name in capitals vertically down the side of the page for the first draft.

Differentiation

Children who need support may only manage the first draft as in the first example above. The prompt sheet at the end of the chapter is to help them write notes. Most children will move on the next level to extend their poems and make them more interesting. The most able may be able to extend their work by making it rhyme.

Plenary

Children read their poems to the class. Give them the opportunity to suggest improvements.

Link up with other subjects

This can be followed up in art lessons with children drawing pictures to illustrate their neat copies.

Choose a person or race of people they are studying in history and write an acrostic poem about them.

Choose a topic you have studied in geography, such as weather, rivers, mountains and write an interesting acrostic.

ACROSTIC POEMS

Finish each line to make and acrostic poem. You can use the words under the title to help you.

PIG

snorts, hairy, markings, curly tail, snout, trotters, rolls in mud, munches, dirty, piglets

Pink_____

Inky _____

Grunts_____

HEN

clucks, struts, pink bill, thin yellow legs, lays, feathers, flapping wings,

Hens_____

Eggs _____

Nest_____

BUDGIE

yellow, green, red, blue, chirps, words, beak, seeds, water, mirror, cage, flies, flits, swings, hops, speckled

Bright feathers_____

Up the ladder_____

Dips_____

Gives _____

In its cage _____

Eggs _____

Name of person in the acrostic poem_____

To help you make notes fill in the bullet points.

Things he/she is good at

- _____

- _____

- _____

- _____

Things he/she loves

- _____

- _____

- _____

- _____

Things he/she hates

- _____

- _____

- _____

- _____

What he/she does at the

week-end and holidays

- _____

- _____

- _____

Where he/she lives

- _____

- _____

Games, sports or musical instruments

- _____

- _____

- _____

7   CAUTIONARY TALES

In 1907, Hilaire Belloc published his book of humorous cautionary tales. These were melodramatic stories of badly behaved children who come to a sticky end as a result of their misbehaviour. Of course, the stories were often far-fetched and could not be taken seriously, but they can still cause amusement. This is a suitable activity for older Key Stage 2 and Lower Key Stage 3 pupils who have some experience of writing poetry.

Cautionary tales can be any length. Some are a few lines and some are a few pages, so children of all levels of ability can produce a completed cautionary tale. If you type google 'Hilaire Belloc's cautionary tales' you will find lots of websites with examples of funny tales to use to show the children.

Lesson 1

Objective: to examine Cautionary Tales and understand their characteristics;

to write a whole class cautionary tale, using the suggestions provided.

Warm-up

Introduce 'caution' and 'cautionary' and ensure everyone understands the meanings.

Explain the background of Hilaire Belloc's 'Cautionary Tales' as above.

Read a few of the cautionary tales. Using an IWB is a convenient way to present them.

'Henry King' and 'Rebecca' by Hilaire Belloc (copyright, 1907) are reproduced by permission of PFD (www.pfd.co.uk) on behalf of The Estate of Hilaire Belloc.

Henry King

The chief defect of Henry King
Was chewing little bits of string.
At last he swallowed some which tied

Itself in ugly knots inside.
Physicians of the utmost fame
Were called at once; but when they came
They answered, as they took their fees,
'There is no cure for this disease.
Henry will very soon be dead.'
His parents stood about his bed
Lamenting his untimely death,
When Henry, with his latest breath,
Cried, 'Oh, my friends, be warned by me,
That breakfast, dinner, lunch, and tea
Are all the human frame requires..."
With that, the wretched child expires.

Rebecca

Who Slammed Doors For Fun And Perished Miserably

A trick that everyone abhors
In little girls is slamming doors.
A wealthy banker's little daughter
Who lived in Palace Green, Bayswater
(By name Rebecca Offendort),
Was given to this furious sport.
She would deliberately go
And slam the door like billy-o!
To make her uncle Jacob start.
She was not really bad at heart,
But only rather rude and wild;
She was an aggravating child...
It happened that a marble bust
Of Abraham was standing just
Above the door this little lamb
Had carefully prepared to slam,
And down it came! It knocked her flat!
It laid her out! She looked like that.
Her funeral sermon (which was long
And followed by a sacred song)
Mentioned her virtues, it is true,
But dwelt upon her vices too,
And showed the dreadful end of one
Who goes and slams the door for fun.
The children who were brought to hear
The awful tale from far and near
Were much impressed, and inly swore

They never more would slam the door,
As often they had done before.

Hilaire Belloc

Emphasise that Hilaire Belloc's book of entertaining tales was published in 1907 and tells of children of that era. For example, 'JIM' is the tale of a child who paid a dreadful price for the faux pas of leaving his nurse in a crowd. Point out that cautionary tales can be written in the present era, reflecting the world we live in today, like the following.

Natasha

Natasha was a spiteful kid.
No matter what the children did,
She was there to spoil their games.
She pulled their hair and called them names.
With adults she was always rude.
She had such ghastly attitude.
Many kids were sorely vexed,
When she sent out a nasty text.

When they opened their emails,
You'd cringe to hear their cries and wails.
She kicked the boys in the groin
And was known to purloin
Wallets and purses from her mates.
Now, as you know, each child hates
To be the victim of the bully.
Natasha was only ever fully
Satisfied when causing harm.
She loved to frighten and alarm.

She picked on little Charlotte Grainger
And thrust the poor child into danger.
She shoved her towards a passing car.
This was just one step too far.
The driver, thank goodness, was alert.
And braked so Charlotte wasn't hurt.
He shouted, 'That's a serious assault!
If she'd been killed it would be your fault.
Such crim'nal behaviour, I do detest.'
The driver made a citizen's arrest.
He marched her off to the local nick.
In wrath, he reported her savage trick
To the sergeant who was most outraged.
He very speedily engaged

A lawyer in the criminal court,
To which the girl, in shame, was brought.

Natasha was tried and convicted,
And now in jail she is afflicted
With loneliness and misery
And no one gives her sympathy.
So, bullies, beware of violent crime.
Or you will spend years serving time.   H. A. Bennett

Charlie Smoke

This ugly lout called Charlie Smoke
Was such a vile, unhealthy bloke.
His clothes were always soiled and shoddy.
He never bothered to wash his body.

For breakfast he drank cans of coke
And so many cakes they made him choke.
For lunch, each day, his mum would give
Him lots of snacks with e-additive.
The bags of sweets and piles of chips
Built up fat on his legs and hips.
All his friends would wail and moan,
'You're overweight by three stone.'

Reverend Green said, 'Think of your ticker.'
He scoffed and swore at the vicar.
He took up two seats on the bus.
If asked to move along, he'd cuss.

Ignoring every kindly warning,
On his way to work each morning,
He puffed away, fag after fag,
And after every single drag,

Blew smelly smoke-rings everywhere,
Even into ladies' hair.
He was proud to be procosious
And his manners were atrocious.

He very heavily hit the bottle
And loudly swore that he would throttle
Any landlord who would bar him.
Even said he'd punch and scar him.
Eventually he was diabetic.
Of course, his end was pathetic.

A life of drink and cakes and smoke
Brought about an early stroke.
His mother watched him, dewy-eyed,
As Charlie breathed his last and died.   H.A Bennett

Discuss their characteristics.

- The title is the name of the villain.

- Melodramatic

- The child's misdemeanours are many and greatly exaggerated.

- The punishment is ghastly and gruesome.

- The poem is written in rhyming couplets and occasionally 3 rhyming lines.

- Each line of the poem has 4 feet.

- The stress is usually on the 2nd, 4th, 6th and 8th syllable.

Main part

Planning a class cautionary tale

- Children choose a character - decide whether it will be man, woman, boy or girl.

- Brainstorm ideas on what his misbehaviour is. Write a list of 'crimes'. It might look like the example below.

    Boy –   flouts all the instructions of parents and teachers

            cheats at school,

            steals other children's homework,

            spoils children's art work - destroys their models, throws paint

            on pictures,

            pinches other children's food,

- Think up an appropriate name for him. It is effective to choose a name which reflects the personality – e.g. Harry Steal, Pete Cheat.

- Decide what was his punishment, e.g.

            expelled from school,

            no school will take him and so he is lonely and homesick in a borstal,

            the children give him some violent punishment which kills him.

Often when writing poetry, children have lots of ideas but they are impeded by trying to make it rhyme, so show them how to prepare a set of rhymes before they start. Write down each crime and ask the class to brainstorm suggestions for rhyming words. The plan below works well for me.

Misdemeanours	Rhyming words
flouts all the instructions of parents and teachers	bad lad mad
	screechers teachers
	destruction instruction
	school fool rule
cheats at school,	steal squeal shirk work irk
steals other children's homework,	smashed trashed splashed
	painted fainted
spoils children's art work	enjoyed destroyed
	should, never good
destroys their models, throws paint on pictures,	lunch crunch punch
	cool school
pinches other children's food,	
expelled from school	

Ask children to suggest rhyming couplets to write the class tale, using their notes. Write them on your board or type them onto an IWB as you go along.

Plenary

Read their poem in unison. Ask them to say which parts they think work well and which could be improved. Read couplets individually to see if they have four beats. Suggest rewording to improve the rhythm.

Tell them to think up a nasty character for their next lesson.

Lesson 2

Objective: to write their own cautionary tale

Warm-up

Read again a cautionary tale and revise characteristics of it.

Main part

Children write their notes for their own cautionary tale, using the model from Lesson 1, working either in pairs or singly. Then they start composing their tale. Getting the metre right is difficult for children, so tell them to concentrate on the ideas and the rhyming couplets. To begin, it does not matter if the rhythm is not an exact four beats in a line, or tetrameter.

Differentiation

Children, who need support, can use the notes from lesson 1 and fill in the skeleton poem at the end of the chapter, or use the alternative notes and skeleton plan provided on the last three pages of this chapter. In the skeleton plan, they can change the words which are inserted, leave any pairs of lines out, or better still, insert their own.

Plenary

Read poems out to the class. Invite children to comment on the parts which work well. This is a challenging activity and might need extra sessions to finish the poems.

Link up with other subjects

Follow-up in other lessons by making typed or neat handwritten copies to make a display or class book of illustrated cautionary tales. Alternatively, for your class assembly, read their poems for other children to mime the actions.

Choose a villain from a book they have read and write as short cautionary tale about him or her.

CAUTIONARY TALES

(Skeleton plan of poem for notes from lesson 1)

Name of child   _____

_____ _____ was a _____ lad.

His parents_____ bad.

_____ was _____ son.

He _____ dad and mum.

At school _____ work.

He wanted _____ and shirk.

When children _____ he took

Their _____ book.

After art lessons _____smashed

_____ trashed

He_____ mean

He _____ lego and plasticine.

At lunch-time _____ hurt

When _____dessert.

_____

_____

At last the children _____ 'thief and liar.'

62

And threw _____ bonfire.

Use this plan for a cautionary tale about a nasty girl. You can fill in the blanks with your own ideas. Now think up a name which suits her like Vera Spite or Mena Hurt.

Misdemeanours	Rhyming words
Bullied other children	child wild.
Pushed them out of her way	
Threw children´s belongings down the toilet	loo threw
Destroyed their toys	toys destroys annoyed destroyed
	names games
Spoilt all their games	netball no fun at all
Made hurtful remarks	hit fit
	tyre ire
Let teacher´s car tyres down	glass crass
Broke windows	toil soil planted ranted
Attacked people´s gardens	mess distress
	zoo do you bears dares unawares
Children threw her into the bear pit	

(Skeleton plan for cautionary tale about a nasty girl)

Name of child _____

_____ _____ was a _____ child.

She _____ wild.

When lining up,_____ rush

To _____ push.

One day _____ threw

Other _____ loo.

In the yard _____ games

She _____ names.

To her teacher _____rude

And _____ attitude.

She _____ car tyre

And laughed_____ire

_____

_____

On _____ zoo

_____ said 'We're _____you.'

They _____ unawares

And _____ pit of bears.

8   CHRISTMAS CARD RHYMES

Nowadays, often only better quality Christmas cards contain a verse to accompany the greeting. In the fortnight approaching Christmas, children love to make cards and this is a lovely opportunity to combine an enjoyable activity with some poetry writing to make a more impressive item. Making cards on a desktop publisher and typing in their verse is a stimulating activity.

Choose one of the following – acrostic, haiku, cinquain, alliteration, enjambment. You might find it helpful to read the chapter on each before you start.

Lesson plan

Objective: to write a short verse for a Christmas card.

Warm-up

Read out some verses from previous years' Christmas cards, if you can find them. Ask children to comment on the characteristics of verses you get in Christmas cards.

- a pleasant, happy tone
- short and to the point
- different styles

Main Part (choose one of the five for each lesson.)

1   **An acrostic verse**

Introduce the term 'acrostic' by reading the examples below. It is best if the children can see them written down.

Magi
Making their way
Along the dry, dusty desert to bring
Gifts of gold, frankincense and myrrh to the
Infant King.

Santa
Sleigh, full of gifts
Along the
Night sky
Taking gifts to
All the children.

Explain that an acrostic verse does not have to rhyme and could be a clause, sentence or description. Ask children to suggest Christmas words – Nativity, holly and ivy, snowman, gifts, robin, carols, parties.

Model it on the board using a Christmas word suggested by the children. Write it on the board, with the letters going down the left hand side of the board. Brainstorm words associated with the word and write them on the right-hand side as the children suggest them. It might look like this.

H

O   hurts your hands
                                                     thorny, shiny leaves
                                                     makes lovely wreaths
L   decorates your home
                                                     grows all year round
L   bright red berries

Y

Invite the children to suggest lines which begin with the letters of the word. Emphasise that although it need not rhyme, it is important to have interesting vocabulary which creates pictures in your mind.

They might, collectively, produce something like this.

Holly
Hurts your hands because
Of its thorns.
Long stems of leaves

Looks pretty in wreaths.
Yields red berries.

Read the acrostic and then encourage them to improve it with adjectives, adverbs, more information. Like this.

Holly
Hurts your hands because
Of its leaves edged with sharp thorns.
Long stems of shiny, dark green leaves
Looks pretty in Christmas wreaths.
Yields bright red berries.

Invite their comments on the improvement.

Using the class example as their model, children write their own acrostic to match the picture on their Christmas card.

2   **A Christmas haiku**

A haiku is a Japanese poem with three lines of five, seven and five syllables. This is a suitable verse to add to the picture on the front of a card. It works well for a scene or a single object.

Introduce the term 'haiku' by reading the examples below. It is best if the children can see them written down.

White Christmas
Gardens covered with
Icing sugar and crystals
Crunching underfoot

Christmas Day
Sweet delicious food
Church bells ringing merrily
Decorated homes

Presents
Beautiful parcels
Ripped open excitedly
Cheers from happy kids

Ask children to identify the characteristics of a haiku.

•   three lines

•   five syllables, seven syllables, five syllables

- does not need to rhyme
- is very descriptive, conjures up a detailed image in few words
- makes good use of senses

Invite each child to suggest a title for a haiku which suits the front picture of his/her card. Write a one or two examples on the board and invite children to suggest phrases to use. Remember to use more than one sense. Use the example below as a model.

Christmas Concert

Choir singing lustily,   buzzing with excitement,   percussion tapping, banging, tinkling   wind booming,   strings pinging, strumming,   poetry, rhythm and rhyme,   Christmas carols,   Christmas spirit,   happy parents

Invite the children to suggest lines of five or seven syllables using their suggestions above. Emphasise that interesting words are important, and unimportant words like 'a' and 'the' can be cut out by using plurals.

When the class has composed a haiku collectively, most should be able to compose one of their own by making their own notes first. The more able can compose a second or third haiku.

3   **A cinquain**

This is another short verse, which is useful to describe the picture on the Christmas card. It has the following pattern.

Line 1:   one word

Line 2:   two words

Line 3:   three words

Line 4:   four words

Line 5:   one word

Explain that the cinquain can be written as individual words or in a sentence as long as it follows the pattern.

Invite the children to tell you the pictures on their cards. Choose one and ask them to suggest lots words and phrases to describe it.

Notes for a cinquain about Santa Claus might be like this.

Red coat   red jacket   white trimming   white beard   North Pole   reindeer
Rudolph   sacks full of toys   sleigh   all over the world

Then ask them to suggest lines in the pattern. They might compose some thing like this.

Santa
Red suit
Reindeer pulling sleigh
Bringing games, sweets, toys
Everywhere

Notes for a cinquain about a nativity scene might look like this

Mary   Joseph   Baby Jesus   stable   animals   oxen   donkey
shepherds   manger   cradle   tired   star

Jesus
King born
In a stable
Mary, Joseph, oxen, donkeys
Watching

Cinquains can also be written in the pattern of

Line 1:   a noun

Line 2:   two adjectives

Line 3:   three action words ending in –ing words

Line 4:   a phrase, any number of words

Line 5:   a word for the noun in line 1

Make notes on the picture of your Christmas card. Use them to write a cinquain following the pattern above. Notes for a picture of an attractive Christmas tree might look like this

fairy lights   twinkle   sparkle   bells   shiny balls   angel
tinsel   glitter   gold   silver   red   green   pine needles
pretty   pleasant   lovely

Christmas tree
shiny, pleasant
Glittering, sparkling, twinkling
Pretty decorations to brighten up the living room
lovely

4   Use alliterations to make a Christmas verse. It does not have to rhyme.

To get ideas ask the children to brainstorm ideas of all the activities that take place in

preparation for Christmas. Make notes like this.

baking	cakes, mince pies, yule logs, plum pudding
buying	presents, cards, fancy table cloths, napkins, stockings, nuts, fruit
wrapping	gifts, presents,
putting up	tree, decorations, cards
writing	cards, labels
going to	parties, church,
listening to	carols, Christmas songs
waiting for	Santa Claus, visitors
opening	cards, Advent calendars, gifts
making	calendars, cards, cakes
decorating	shiny bells and baubles, tinsel, angel, fairy, paper chains, holly wreath

Pick out alliterative words and phrases. Put in adjectives and adverbs to extend the

alliteration. Put them together to build up an attractive picture of Christmas.

Bells and baubles shining brightly,
Tinsel and lights twinkling on the tree,
Plum pudding, mince pies,
Singing Christmas carols merrily.
Signs that Christmas time is here.

or

Writing cards and wrapping presents,
Christmas carols with sweet singing,
Awaiting Santa Claus, Advent calendars
These are joys that Christmas is bringing.

5   Write a two-lined enjambment greeting for Christmas and the following year. An

enjambment contains a sentence which rolls from one line to the next. Ask children to tell

70

you what they would wish for other people. Write them in a column and then ask them to add rhyming words which you could use to make a friendly greeting. Look up a rhyming dictionary for words you can use.

peace	increase	release
happiness	bless	success
good health	wealth	
prosperity	tree	be
fun	begun	
love	above	

Put the two rhyming words at the end and fill in the line. They might produce lines like this.

I hope this year will bless
You with love and happiness.

Best wishes for a year of health
Happiness, success and wealth.

I hope you have lots of gifts round your tree
And a year of health and prosperity.

I hope for you this year will be
Full of fun and gaiety.

Plenary

Children read their poems out for children to say what they like about them or suggest improvements.

As a final whole class activity, ask children to suggest a follow-on line for each of these.

Christmas is a special time

_____

Chiming bells and carol singing

_____

Church bells ring on Christmas morning

_____

9   CINQUAINS

Cinquains are another good starting point for pupils who believe they cannot write poetry. They like them because they do not have to rhyme. They are a form of poetic verse which follows a pattern of five lines. Like haikus they force writers to focus their minds on putting as much meaning as possible into very few words. There are different patterns for writing cinquains. The simplest pattern is

Line 1:   one word

Line 2:   two words

Line 3:   three words

Line 4:   four words

Line 5:   one word.

Cinquains have no title but the first line serves as a title.

Lesson 1

Objective: to understand the characteristics of simple cinquains and write whole class examples

Warm up

Read out some cinquains like those below. Let the pupils see them written down.

Holidays
No school
Family trips abroad
Playing with friends merrily
Brilliant

School
Hard work
Lots to learn
Maths, English, History, Geography,
Interesting

Romans
Invaded Britain,
Building roads, towns
Villas, shops, baths amphitheatres
expertly.   H. A .Bennett

Ask the pupils to tell you the main characteristics of a cinquain. Make sure they have noted these points

•   five lines

•   pattern of one, two, tree, four, one words

•   lots of information in a few words.

•   can be descriptive or a sentence written in the pattern.

Main part

Ask children to suggest a popular game or toy. Ask them to suggest words and phrases which this game/toy puts into their heads and write as many as you can on your board or type onto your IWB.

For a game of Twister, they might suggest

family fun   brightly coloured circles   spinners   falling all over the place

funny   laughing   hands and feet   awkward positions   great fun white

sheet

Remind them of the pattern of a cinquain – one word, two words, three words, four words, one word. Make sure that everyone understands how the poem fits the pattern. Then point out all of their notes about 'Twister' or other game and one line at a time, ask for suggestions for a cinquain on 'Twister'.

Write the class cinquain on the board with words and phrases which the pupils suggest. They will probably suggest something like this.

Twister
A sheet
Spin the spinner
Family laughing, falling over
Funny

Usually a cinquain can be improved. Ask the children to look at it again. Emphasise these points.

- They only have 11 words to use, so it is better not to use words like 'a' and 'the'.

- The more information they put into their 11 words, the more powerful it is.

- A strong verb is better than a verb and adverb, or a verb and preposition

Ask pupils to improve their class cinquain. The above cinquain could be improved like this.

Twister
White sheet
Coloured circles, spinner
Family playing, tumbling, laughing,
Funny

Invite the pupils to comment on the effect of the changes they have made.

Pupils, in pairs or singly, choose their own game or toy and write notes and write their own cinquain.

Differentiation

Pupils who need support can work with a more able writer to scribe their ideas.

Plenary

Pupils read their cinquains to the class. Encourage pupils to comment on what is effective or powerful in each other´s poems.

Lesson 2

In preparation, ask each pupil to bring in a piece of fruit or a vegetable. It is best for teachers to bring in a few as well.

Objective: to write a more complicated cinquain

to use a theasaurus

Warm-up:

Ask pupils to remind you of the pattern – one, two, three, four, one word per line.

Show them these cinquains.

Rugby
Lively, fast
Running, passing, scoring
Adrenaline running through strong lads
Terrific!

Rounders
Competitive, exciting
Bowling, batting, scoring
Whole class enjoys it
Fun   H. A. Bennett

Ask them to point out the pattern. Check that they have included these.

Line 1:   a noun

Line 2:   two adjectives

Line 3:   three –ing action words

Line 4:   a phrase with any number of words

Line 5:   a word for the noun in line 1

Main part

Show children how to use a thesaurus. Introduce the word 'synonym' Give them a few words to practice finding synonyms.

Pass the fruit and vegetables round and ask pupils to feel the surface, sniff them, think of words to describe the appearance and think of the taste. Remind them of similes, metaphors, alliteration. Brainstorm words to describe the fruits and vegetables. Remind them to use sight, smell, feel and taste.

Pupils then choose one fruit or vegetable each and write down their words and phrases for it.

Choose one to be the model and ask the pupils to suggest words and phrases in the pattern above.

For example

Banana
Yellow, smooth
Peeling, biting, munching
A break-time snack
Nice

Whatever pupils suggest, you can usually improve it. Suggest replacing 'a', 'the' and uninteresting words like 'nice,' 'good', 'bad'. Remind them to think of words which describe feelings. Pupils could suggest improvements like the one below.

Banana
Yellow, smooth,
Peeling, biting, munching
Sweet, satisfying break-time snack
Delicious

Pupils use the notes they have made to write their own cinquain. Encourage them to use the thesaurus to find more interesting vocabulary, and to use as many senses as they can.

Differentiation

Pupils who need support use the prompt sheet below to make notes to organise their ideas. The first is completed for them to use as an example. Pupils who finish quickly can choose another topic, for example, their favourite meal on which to write notes and a cinquain.

Pineapple

Look	Yellow, beige, thin, green leaves, pimply
Feel	Rough, diamond shaped pattern, crunchy inside, juicy
Smell	Fresh,
Taste	delicious, tasty, sweet
How does it make you feel?	satisfied, no longer thirsty

Look	
Feel	
Smell	
Taste	
How does it make you feel?	

Plenary

Put pupils into mixed groups of three or four and give each group a subject which the class has not yet discussed and give them ten minutes to write to group cinquain with one person in each group scribing for the others. You should get lots of ideas if you suggest topics such as ice-cream, lollipops, chocolate, trifle, gateau, jam tarts, lemon meringue pie. Read their cinquains to the class.

Lesson 3

Objective: to write cinquains based on a syllable count of two, four, six, eight, two syllables

Warm-up:

Recap on what makes an effective cinquain – interesting vocabulary, senses, using few words to give most information. Show how a sentence can be cut down to give the same information. Use this example.

The Vikings were very good at sailing and they found lots of foreign lands which they had never seen before.   (14 words)

Skilful sea-faring Vikings discovered many new lands.   (7 words)

Invite pupils to show how the same information was conveyed in half as many words. Discuss how it was done – using an adjective 'skilful' to replace the phrase 'were very good at sailing' and the adjective 'new' to replace the relative clause 'which they had never seen before'.

Give the pupils, in pairs, a copy of the sheet on the next page to reduce the sentences into short concise sentences. This can be done orally or in writing.

CINQUAINS

TOO MANY WORDS

Pick out the most important words and make these sentences shorter, keeping in all the information. Try to make the word count shorter than the number in brackets.

1.   If you put a lot of salt into water, stir it round and round and then heat it, all of the salt will disappear.   (24 words)

_____

_____

2   Kenya is a country in East Africa, where the people grow maize, coffee and bananas, and they send them abroad to sell to other countries.   (25 words)

_____

_____

3   The Celts first began coming to Britain round about six or seven hundred years before Christ and they brought iron to Britain.(22 words)

_____

_____

4   If you cannot find the colour you want in art lessons, you can make your colour by mixing other colours and adding a little touch of white to make it a lighter shade. (33 words)

_____

_____

5   In technology lessons it is important to handle tools carefully, in the way you have been shown, in order to avoid nasty accidents. (23 words)

_____

_____

6   In music lessons you can enjoy yourself by joining in a variety of activities using percussion instruments and singing. (19 words)

_____

_____

Main part

Introduce the cinquains below.

Wasps flit
Among flowers.
Flying football jerseys,
Nature's friends pollinate, punish
With stings

Sports day
Pupils happy,
Eager to win events,
Hurdle, throw, jump, sprint to the line.
Healthy

H. A. Bennett

Explain the meaning of 'syllable'. Ask pupils to point out the pattern. Check that they have these points. Prompt them to count the syllables, if necessary, and write the pattern on the board as an aide-memoire.

Line 1:   two syllables

Line 2:   four syllables

Line 3:   six syllables

Line 4:   eight syllables

Line 5:   two syllables

•   lots of ideas in very few words

•   made up of a mixture of words, phrases and sentences

•   a mixture of descriptions and actions

If pupils have tried one or both of the other types of cinquain, most should be able to make notes and write their own to edit and improve.

Differentiation

Give the children this prompt sheet to get their ideas flowing. Change the titles or use the ones below.

Football

What is it?	
What happens?	
How does it make you feel?	
Where do you go for it?	

Computer games

What are they?	
What happens?	
How does it make you feel?	
Where do you go for it?	

Plenary to link up with other subjects

Put children into groups or pairs and ask them to choose a topic from another subject. E.g. geography, rivers; or science, a piece of scientific equipment like a Bunsen burner, and write a group cinquain. Read them to the class.

10   CLERIHEWS

A clerihew is a verse of four lines, written to describe a person. Children love them because the lines are humorous and sometimes nonsensical, so they are amusing, and fun to write.

They are named after Edmund Clerihew Bentley, who invented them. If you google 'Clerihew' you will find lots of examples.

Lesson plan

Objective: to understand the format of a clerihew and compose a class clerihew.

Warm-up

Introduce the term 'clerihew' and give a few examples, like these.

Our silly teacher Mrs Bennett
Went mad yesterday, when it
Occurred to her that it was past three,
So she'd missed her afternoon cup of tea.

We have a clever teacher Miss Shaw
Who, when relaxing, loves to draw.
She drew a cartoon of the headmaster.
He felt insulted, such a disaster.

Our biology teacher, Mr Jones,
Is so thin he's a bag of bones.
He's so grumpy, the children all hate him.
He kicked some dogs and they ate him.

Our games teacher Mr Smith
Loved coming to school in his car with
His pet python and anaconda.
They squeezed him and now he is no longer.

Our school caretaker, Mr Gunning
Was a devious man of great cunning.
When cook was out, he stole biscuits and cake

Now he's got raging tummy and toothache.

My old friend Mildred Napeer.
Had too may fags and too much beer.
She ignored the advice everyone gave
So now poor Millie's in her grave.

This is the tale of Percy Pars
Who was fond of speedy cars.
Always wanting to drive faster
His last journey was a disaster.

My great auntie, Rena Remicles
Loved to play with dangerous chemicals
She mixed them up and shook them round.
It all exploded and her house fell down.   H. A. Bennett

Ask the children to tell you the characteristics of a clerihew. Check that they have deduced these points.

- A verse with 4 lines

- The last words on the first and second lines rhyme and the last words on the third and fourth lines rhyme. Introduce the term aabb.

- The first line ends with the name of the person about whom the poem is written or where they come from.

- The last word of the second line rhymes with the name of the person.

- The verse is funny, sometimes nonsensical.

- The lines can be of different lengths so there does not have to be standard rhythm.

Main part

Ask children to suggest names and write a few examples in a column on the left-hand side of the board. Brainstorm rhyming words for each and add them. Point out that a word with lots of rhyming partners will be easier to use for a rhyming couplet. Remind pupils of how to use a rhyming dictionary and encourage them to use it. The board might look like this.

Janet	planet
Tom	bomb,
James	names, games, shames, frames, blames, tames
Anna	banana, piranha
Rosie	dozy, posy, nosy,
Mrs Hay}	grey, day, say, pray, way, stay, may, obey
Mr Gray}	bay, affray, lay, neigh, pay, ray, slay display
Auntie Mary	canary, hairy, fairy, wary, berry, dairy
Mandy	candy, handy, sandy, bandy, brandy
Nicky	tricky, sickie, picky

Choose one name and ask the children to suggest two funny lines to start. Choose a pair and write it on the board. Then ask children to think of two lines to follow on from it. You might get something like these.

> There was a young lad called Tom
> Who was determined to make a bomb.
> He worked in his shed, with his brains and his wits
> But now Tom and his shed are in bits.

> There was a young woman called Janet
> Who rocketed off to another planet.
> Her spaceship vanished without a trace
> So Janet is floating forever in space.

Children work, in pairs or singly, to write their own notes or use the notes on the board to write their own clerihews.

Differentiation
Children who need support can use the skeleton sheet on the next page to get them started.

Plenary
Present these two lines to the class and give the children five minutes to think up two funny finishing lines and recite them to the class.

I have a pet pteradactyl called Terry.
He's full of fun and loves to be merry.

Link up with other subjects

Choose a character you are studying in history and write a clerihew about him/her.

Look up Edmund Clerihew Bentley in books, encyclopaedias or the Internet and read about him. Write a few paragraphs about him.

CLERIHEWS

Auntie Mary

My _____ Auntie Mary

_____ yellow canary.

She _____ every day.

The canary _____ and flew away.

Rosie

I _____called Rosie,

Who _____ dozy

In _____ she fell asleep

And made _____ and weep.

Lily

_____called Lily

Who loved _____

She _____ one day

And now _____. frilly,

hilly, chilli, chilly, fusilli, Millie, Billy, piccalilli

May

I knew _____ May.

Who _____

_____

_____

Rhyming words to use for line 2

say, play, day, sway, grey, clay, hay, lay, stay, away

11   ENJAMBMENT POEMS

Enjambment poems are poems in which the sentences continue into the next line. John Keats used the technique in his delightful poem 'A thing of beauty'. They can have any rhyme scheme, for example, aabb, abcb, aabbc.

Writing enjambment poems which rhyme is easier than it looks, because you can put your rhyming words anywhere in a sentence and then manoeuvre them to the end of the line.

Lesson plan

Objective: to understand the characteristics of enjambment and write a class poem using enjambment.

Warm up

Explain the term 'enjambment' and read the verses below. It is best if the children can see the words so that they can see how the sentence carries on from one line to the next.

A thing of beauty is a joy for ever:
Its loveliness increases; it will never
Pass into nothingness; but still will keep
A bower quiet for us, and a sleep
Full of sweet dreams, and health, and quiet breathing.   John Keats

I once saw a barrier of billboards where someone had painted on this rhyme.
I think that I shall never see
A billboard, lovely as a tree.
I think unless the billboards fall
I'll never see a tree sat all.   Anon.

In his book, NOW WE ARE SIXTY, Christopher Matthew, used the same technique to write a book of humorous poems. These poems are reproduced with the kind permission of Christopher Matthew.

SIR JOHN'S FANCY

Sir John was quite a vain man -
He liked his share of praise.
When people didn't speak to him,
He'd sulk for days and days.
And when he put his gear on
And jogged around the park,
He wouldn't go when it was light,
He said he thought it wasn't right,
His lycra shorts were much too tight -
He went when it was dark.

STREET THEATRE

Wherever I go
My mouth's like an 'O'
Because life is so full of surprises.
When I walk down the street
I am certain to meet
Performers in various guises.

WRINKLIES

When Viv and I go to the shops
For milk and bread and cheese and chops,
We look at all the wrinklies there,
Who shuffle around the shelves and stare,

And tell ourselves when we are old
Our hands won't shake, we won't lose hold.
And when we're halfway home we find
We've left the cheese and chops behind.   Christopher Matthew

Invite the children's comments on the poems and check that they have got the following points.

•   The sentences lead from one line into the next line or onto the next verse.

•   The verses can have any rhyme scheme.

- The verses can be humorous or serious.

Also note that there is alliteration in 'cheese and chops' and make sure that pupils understand that 'wrinklies' means old people.

Main part

Depending on the class, the activities below might run into one, two or three lessons.

To write an enjambment poem, you can start by writing long sentences with rhyming words and fit them into verses later. Choose a topic, for example, the seaside.

Ask children to suggest 'seaside' words and write/type them down the left-hand side of the board/IWB. Remind them to uses their senses and techniques like alliteration.

Now think of lots of rhyming words which you could associate with the seaside and other suitable words to go into sentences with them.

boat,	float,			
ice-cream,	scene			
ship,	trip			
swim,	skim			
promenade,	lad,	Grandad		
sand,	land,	planned		
sun	fun,	run,	begun,	everyone
beach	each			
picnic	stick of rock			
spade	wade,	played,	shade, stayed, parade
seaweed	feed,	lead,	need	
rock pool	full			
seagulls	squawking,	talking		
salty air,	fair			
waves,	caves			
fizzy drinks,	busy,	dizzy,		

In order to get the words and ideas flowing, ask the children, in pairs or singly, to use these words, and others to write random sentences about a trip to the seaside. Ask them to read their sentences round the class. Emphasize that the rhyming words above do not need to go at the end of the sentence, because lots of final words in the line will be mid-sentence. Write/type up as many as you can on your board/IWB. It might look like this.

> We spent ages building castles with our buckets and spades.
>
> We found a rock pool that had lots of tiddlers and crabs.
>
> We had a lot of fun running races across the beach.
>
> You could smell the salt in the air.
>
> We bought a stick of rock to take home to Grandad.
>
> We bought soft ice-cream on the promenade.
>
> I got dizzy in the rides in the funfair.
>
> We played frisbee on the beach.
>
> We could see lots of sailing boats and ships on the horizon.
>
> We had a picnic on the beach.
>
> Seagulls landed on the sand looking for leftovers of picnics

Now ask the children to think up an interesting opening pair of enjambment lines to start the poem. They do not need to rhyme. For example,

> Last week our class went to Southend
> On a coach for a summer trip.

Ask children to brainstorm quite a long sentence ending in a rhyming word for the last word in the last line, in this case, ´trip´. For example,

> In the horizon we could see
> An enormous cross channel ship.

Now use your rhyming words and sentences to make enjambment lines for the poem. Point out that they can be rhyming couplets like this

> We smelt the salty sea air
> As we had our rides at the fair

Or they can have sets of 4 lines with the second and fourth lines rhyming or any other rhyme scheme.

> We saw crabs and starfish and tiny tiddlers
> Skittering around in a shallow pool.

We collected water in our buckets
And poured it in until it was full.

Differentiation

The sheet at the end of the chapter can be used as a prompt sheet for those who need learning support.

Plenary

For further practice, read out these lines, one at a time, and challenge the children to add an interesting enjambment line. If they find it difficult, suggest the rhyming lines at the end.

One evening I was in the park

dark, lark,

spark, shark

_____

A dinosaur went out one day

play, stay, way

tray, hay, jay,

_____

Walking in the woods, one night

fright, delight,

sight, right,

_____

We went out into the playground

sound, round,

around, bound,

frowned, pound

_____

One night a spaceship landed there

fair, stare, dare

scare, glare, pair

_____

To link up with other subjects

Choose a character whom you are studying in R.E. and write notes about him/her. Use the notes to write a short enjambment poem.

ENJAMBMENT POEMS

Fill in the blanks to write your own poems. You can change any words on the page and put in your own.

The Seaside

Last week our class went to Southend
On a coach for a summer trip.

We played _____

And we went _____ the sea.

We built _____

And _____ our frisbee.

We _____

And _____ the promenade

To _____

And bought _____for Grandad.

We had a picnic _____

_____ in the shade

The children _____

_____ played.

Our teacher _____

We could feel the breeze _____ salty air

And hear _____

We went off _____ funfair.

We went on _____

And _____dizzy.

_____

_____ sweets and drinks all fizzy.

When we were _____

And _____ on the way home.

12 HAIKUS

A haiku is a Japanese poem of three lines and seventeen syllables. It has the formula

five syllables

seven syllables

five syllables

Normally the words give a description of the title. Sometimes haikus are written with a different number of syllables, but for the purpose of this chapter, I shall stick to the traditional form. When writing haikus, it is best to concentrate on interesting ideas first, and then getting the syllable count right. Like cinquains, writing haikus is a great activity for grasping the skill of expressing yourself succinctly.

Children who need support often find the hardest part is getting started. The differentiated sheets at the end of the chapter give children a start, and practice in fine tuning the words to make them into a haiku, before they try their own.

Writing haikus is a great idea for a lesson if you get a sudden unexpected fall of snow or a heatwave.

Lesson plan

Objective: to understand the form of a haiku and write some interesting haikus

Warm-up

Explain the meaning of haiku and read the following examples.

Tiger
Stripy, fierce creature
Hungrily striding, stalking
Strikes with lightning speed

Sea
Ripply surfaces
Washing soft tropical sand

Relief from hot sun

Sea
Intimidating
High waves pound and devastate
Coastline eroded

Chips
Soft, oily fingers
Hot, tasty vinegar-drenched
Hunger satisfied

Rose
Delicate petals
Scented pinks, lemons and reds
Cruel jagged thorns

Daffodils
Rich green shoots foretell
Spring in pretty yellow bells.
Sweet pollen for bees   H. A. Bennett

Ask for children's reactions to the language.

Make sure they note the main points.

- The lines should describe the title.

- The language should be descriptive and create a picture in the mind.

- The lines are phrases, not necessarily sentences.

- You have very few words to use, so try not to waste them with words like 'a' and 'the'. Sometimes you can avoid the indefinite article by making nouns plural.

- The more ideas you can get into the haiku the more powerful it is.

Main part

To demonstrate how to write a haiku, ask children to name things which they like and choose a few examples to expand. Write a suggestion on the board and invite descriptive words and phrases for it like the suggestion below.

Wii   - smashing fun, play against my family, racquet games in the living room, skiing on the carpet, competitions, golf driving, sports, on TV screen

Now ask the children to suggest lines of five or seven syllables. Tell them that initially, it does not matter if they do not get the syllable count right. They can make suggestions, write them and then work on the syllable count when they are satisfied with their ideas, like this.

A first try, just to get ideas might look like this.

Wii
Hours of family fun
Outdoor games in the living room
Tennis, golf and ski-ing

In this, the ideas are good but it needs fine tuning to get the syllable count right and put ideas into a more logical order, so invite the class to make suggestions to improve it like the example below.

Second try, to get things into good order and correct the syllable count.

Tennis, golf, ski-ing
Outdoor sports on screen at home
Great family fun

You can repeat the process with other topics which the children suggest.

Seasons are a great starting point. Choose winter, spring, autumn, or summer for the children to make their own notes. The sheets below are for those who need learning support.

Plenary

Children read their haiku for the others to guess the title

To link up with other subjects.

Challenge children to write a haiku about

a game of hockey/football/netball, or

a computer, or

a recent school trip, or

a drama lesson, or

anything they enjoy in school.

HAIKUS
Winter

Write winter words and phrases. Try to think of interesting alliterations and similes and create a picture in your mind. For example, frost like icing sugar.

Weather - snow, ice _____

Days become _____nights are _____

Trees become _____

Hazards - burst pipes, ice on road _____

Animals going into hibernation _____

Winter clothes - scarves _____

Look at this and make it into a haiku. Get rid of the unwanted syllables and you will be surprised how much better each sounds.

Winter

Short days nights get longer
Scarves and hats for frosty mornings
Hedgehogs go in hibernation

Winter

_____

_____

_____

Now use your notes to write your own haiku.

Summer

Write interesting summer words and phrases. Try to think of an expression which creates a picture in your mind. For example, splashes of garden colour. Can you put in a metaphor or an alliteration?

Weather – sunny _____

Days grow _____ nights _____

Trees become _____

Gardens - roses like _____

Summer clothes – sandals _____

Hazards – sunburn _____

Look at this and try to improve it. Get the syllable count right 5,7,5. You can change the words if you can think up a better way of saying things or something more suitable to go with the rest of the haiku.

Summer
Roses lupins and foxgloves
Lovely long days and short nights
Trips to the seaside

_____

_____

_____

Tee-shirts and swimsuits
Take our buckets and spades to the beach
Hours playing every day

_____

_____

_____

Now try your own haiku about summer.

Autumn

Write some interesting autumn words and phrases. Try to think of expressions which create a picture in your mind. For example, leaves like flame.

Weather – mist _____

Days become _____ nights are _____

Trees lose _____

Gardens _____

Animals getting ready for hibernation _____

Clothes - scarves _____

Colours _____

Look at these haikus and try to improve them. Get the syllable count right five, seven, five. You can change the words if you can think up a better way of saying things.

Leaves turn yellow and orange
Fallen leaves cover up the grass
Branches are bare

_____

_____

_____

Winds becoming colder
Sun is getting lower in the sky
Darkness falls earlier

_____

_____

_____

Now write your own haiku about Autumn.

Spring

Add ideas of your own on the lines.

Green shoots, spring flowers – snowdrops, _____

Grass _____ trees _____

Animals coming out of hibernation – tortoise _____

Changes in the countryside – lambs born, tadpoles _____

_____

Air is becoming _____ , days becoming _____

_____

Now use your notes to write your own Haiku.

Spring

_____

_____

_____

Count the syllables and see if they are correct. Can you put in any more interesting words to improve your haiku?

_____

_____

_____

13 KENNINGS

List poems lead on to kennings which are an amusing way to write a poem in a puzzle.

A kenning is a pre-mediaeval type of poem from the Anglo-Saxon era. Each line is a phrase of about two words which replaces the common noun in the title. Pupils can make kenning puzzles. They do not have to rhyme, but it is more satisfying for pupils if they do.

Here are some examples.

Butterfly
Pretty winger
Gentle flutterer
Pollen collector
Nectar detector

Ladybird
Aphid eater
Spotted flier
Beady eyed
Silent treader

Computer
Information processor
Envelope addresser
Table organizer
Information finder
Illustration provider
Greetings card designer
Hyperlink creator
Email sender
Interactive player

H. A. Bennett

Lesson plan

Warm up

Read the kennings above without the titles for pupils to guess what they are.

Discuss what makes up a line of a kenning – about two words per line, usually at least one is a noun, to describe the title.

Main part

Ask the children to choose a topic, a common noun, and write it on your board. Children suggest words associated with it to use as in the example below. Encourage children to use as many senses as possible as in the example below.

> Wasp – stripes, flier, buzzer, stinger, nest, carries pollen, pyjamas, flits, football jersey, flies to pretty flowers, frightens people, legs like thread, lays eggs

Now use the notes to make lines of a kenning with class brainstorming ideas. Write them on the board as they call them out. Remind them that each line must describe the title. They might produce something like this.

> Stripy flier
> Nest occupier
> Nasty stinger
> Pain bringer
> Pyjamas wearer
> Pollen bearer
> Egg layer

Children can work individually, or in pairs, to write one or two common nouns and after each one, their list of words to use in their kenning. They then use their notes to compose their kennings.

Differentiation

For children who find it difficult to get started, use the two pages at the end of the chapter. The more able can improve their kenning by making it rhyme.

Plenary

The children read their kennings to the class, without the title, for the other children to work out what it is.

To link with other subjects

Choose an object, person or race of people from another topic to write a kenning.

Use their ICT skills to find out about the origin of Kennings.

KENNINGS

Use the words below to fill in the blanks to make your own kenning. You can change the words or put in some of your own. Try to add some lines of your own.

Footballer

exercise, training, matches, team, game, pitch, club, fitness, healthy,

player, header,

treader, scorer, shooter, booter, sweat, tactics

Team _____

Hard _____

Fast _____

Goal _____

Penalty _____

Sharp _____

Fitness _____

Club _____

Keen _____

Tactics _____

_____

_____

_____

_____

Use the words below to fill in the blanks to make your own kenning. You can change the words or put in some of your own. Try to add some lines of your own.

Boat

sea, sails, blowing, steamer, paddle, rowing, oars, rowers, cargo, foam,

cabin, rudders, fishing, carries cargo, engine, oil, crosser, rowing,

deliverer, tosser

sea _____

foam _____

steam _____

spray _____

cargo _____

engine _____

sails _____

oars _____

_____

_____

_____

_____

14   LIMERICKS

These humorous five-lined poems are named after Limerick in Ireland, because they were popular there. However they did not originate there. Variants on the same theme have been written since the 14th century and their form is used in some nursery rhymes, such as Hickory-dickory dock. People made them up for amusement. Because they are short and simple, and often were of a vulgar nature, they once had low status as a poetic form. Edward Lear enhanced their status by including limerick nursery rhymes in his book *A Book of Nonsense*.

If you google 'limericks' you will find thousands of them. Modern limericks usually end their first line with the person's name or a sentence about them. You can use these examples.

An outlaw called Robin Hood
Would never do what he should.
He was much too willing
To go robbing and killing.
The fellow was far, far from good.

James Cook was a great seaman they say.
For he discovered Botany Bay.
When his ship came near grief
On a barrier reef
He skilfully got her away.   John Warren

A clever young student called John
Was so bright they made him a Don.
He never forgot
Anything he was taught.
While with some, an hour later, it's gone.

There was a young lady from Kew
Who was terribly keen on the zoo.
Though a great deal to pay
She went every day

To see her favourite, the kangaroo.

I one knew a friendly emu,
Who lived in a greenhouse in Kew.
He had many a laugh
With the gardeners and staff
And his very best friend was a gnu.   Sheila Jones

There was a young lady from Stroud
Whose voice was horribly loud.
People got sick of her.
All had a kick of her.
She has bruises of which she is proud.

There was a young lady called Rose
Who had a terribly big nose.
Each time she blew it
A shiver went through it
Vibrating right down to her toes.

A lady called Stella McVickers
Loved wearing posh, fancy knickers
Skimpy ones, frilly pairs
Silky thongs, silly pairs,
She covered them all with gold stickers

There was a young man from Barry
Who swore he would never marry.
He stayed fat and unkempt
So no girl would attempt
To take on such a burden to carry.   Hazel Bennett

Lesson Plan

Objective: to understand the structure of limericks and write them

Warm up

Read some limericks to the class and invite their comments. Ask them to tell you what

makes a limerick. Make sure they note these points. Write them on the board.

- 	5 lines

- 	rhyme scheme is a a b b a - lines 1, 2 and 5 rhyme, lines 3 and 4 rhyme,

- 	lines 1,2, and 5 are longer – 3 feet of 7-10 syllables

- 	lines 3 and 4 are shorter – 2 feet of 5-8 syllables

- they are funny
- rhythm - 2 short syllables between the long or stressed syllables – anapaestic rhythm

Main part

Make a class limerick. Brainstorm names of people and places which have got lots of rhymes to go with them. Emphasise that there is no point in using a name like Hazel which has few rhyming pairs.

From the names suggested, choose one which has a lot of rhyming words and write it on the board. Ask the children to use a rhyming dictionary to find lots of words to rhyme with the name or place name chosen. Emphasise that the wider the range of words chosen the easier it is to make an interesting limerick.

The board might look like this.

Guy – try, by, buy, try, bye-bye, cry, die, eye, fly, dragonfly, fry, high, lie, pie, rye,

apply, shy, spy, nigh, sly, reply, nearby, magpie, butterfly, beautify, horrify, multiply

Ask the children to pick out words which might go together, for example, fly, dragonfly, butterfly, magpie,   beautify, nearby   pie, fry, satisfy

Give the children this frame and ask them to suggest short sentences to fill in the blanks. Remind them to change the rhyming words for lines 3 and 4.

_____ called Guy

Who_____

_____

_____

_____

When the class have composed a limerick collectively, they read it together and then work individually or in pairs to write their own limericks. Encourage them to use a rhyming dictionary and make their list of rhyming words before they start. Remind them that the actions do not need to be realistic. In fact an unlikely tale, is more humorous.

Differentiation

Children who need support have most difficulty in finding words which rhyme. The next pages provide writing frames for children to insert their own ideas.

Plenary

A jolly ten minutes with children entertaining the class with their limericks.

Link up with other subjects

Use their ICT skills to surf the net to find out more about the origin of Limericks.

LIMERICKS

Use these words and rhymes to write your own limericks. You may change the words or use other words of your own.

Fred - bed, said, fed, led, bread, dread, head, street cred, Ned, red, instead,

There was a young lad called Fred

Who _____ head.

He _____

_____

_____

_____

Mary – hairy, fairy, contrary, chary, prairie, airy, ferry, berry, cherry, bury, merry, scary, vary, very, canary, ordinary, imaginary, stationary

_____ Mary

Who _____

She_____

_____

_____

Goole – fool, full, tool, pool, stool, toadstool, bull, pull, wool, cool, school, spoonful, bagful, drool, ghoul, mule, rule, Yule, toadstool, ridicule,

There was an old man from Goole

_____

_____

_____

_____

110

Use these words and rhymes to write your own limericks. You may change the words or use other words of your own.

Galway – away, bay, bray, clay, day, grey, hay, hooray, jay, lay, may, nay, neigh, pay, play, display, prey, pray, ray, say, stay, spray, tray, way, weigh,

_____ from Galway,

_____

_____

_____

_____

Knight – fight, fright, flight, height, might, mite, night, light, moonlight, plight, right, sight, site, campsite, tight, Isle o' Wight, bite, polite, kite, spite, sprite, write, white,

_____ knight

_____

_____

_____

_____

Dean – bean, been, clean, unclean, dry-clean green, keen, mean, preen, queen, canteen, between, seen, unseen, scene, caffeine, Christine, hygiene, eighteen, tambourine, plasticine, tangerine, submarine

_____ Dean

_____

_____

_____

_____

15 LIST POEMS

A list poem is made up of a list of people, creatures or events and one fact about each. There are no rules about length or rhyme. This is a suitable type of poem to use for children to get them started in writing poems which rhyme. When they realize they can make a rhyming poem, it gives them confidence to try a more difficult type of rhyming poem.

Lesson Plan

Objective: to recognize the characteristics of list poems and write their own list poem
(Depending on the age and ability of the class, this might run to a second or third lesson.)

Warm up

Introduce the term 'list poem' and read the list poem below.

Animals in Action
Frogs leap
Spiders creep

Grasshoppers jump
Caterpillars hump

Snakes slide
Eagles glide

Bees sting
Monkeys swing

Rabbits hop
Horses clop

Lions pounce
Kangaroos bounce

Chameleons freeze
Pythons squeeze

Cats stalk
But I just walk   H. A. Bennett

Invite the class to describe the characteristics – short lines, rhyming couplets, one simple theme

Main part

- Round the class ask the children to suggest creatures. Make it as wide as possible by suggesting fictitious creatures, insects, birds, fish and prehistoric reptiles.

- Write the names in a column down the left-hand side of the board until you have about fifteen.

- Ask the children to suggest verbs or phrases to go with them. Make it easy for them by saying they can use movement, noise, young or food. Have several suggestions for each creature.

The class notes on your board might look like this.

Mice	nibble, creep, squeak, bite, run, play, scurry
Whales	swim, glide, spout, blow, spurt, gleam
Snakes	slither, rattle, slide, bite, crush, squeeze
Kangaroos	bounce, hop, jump, bite, carry joeys in their pouch, spring,
Turkeys	gobble, strut, peck, lay eggs,
Bees	buzz, hum, flit, sting
Hedgehogs	snuffle, scurry, gnaw, prickle
Eagles	fly, glide, snatch, catch, squawk, attack, swoop, hunt
Tigers	stalk, hunt, roar, kill, draw blood, have cubs, pounce
Pigs	snore, snort, wallow in mud, grunt, have piglets
Parrots	chatter, talk, fly, play, peck, lay eggs, squawk
Dolphins	jump, glide, dive, eat fish, swim, shine
Rabbits	hop, are furry, have kittens
Crocodiles	stand still, kill, waddle along, have thick skin, snap, bite, swim
Monkeys	chatter, crouch, swing, squabble,

Seals	hobble, shuffle, eat fish, swim, have pups
Dragons	fly, glide, have wings, breathe fire, lash their tails

Pupils, in turn, read the lines so that they can see and hear lots of pairs of words which rhyme. Invite them to use the notes on the board to suggest pairs of two or three word lines which rhyme. Write their rhyming couplets on the board.

The class list poem may look like this.

Seals shuffle
Hedgehogs snuffle
Rabbits are furry
Mice scurry
Kangaroos bounce
Tigers pounce
Monkeys squabble
Turkeys gobble
Eagles hunt
Pigs grunt

Reading their class poem together should let children see how easy it is to make one which rhymes.

Children then write their own notes choosing a few more creatures and adding words to make their own list poems, using the class notes and their own. Sometimes they produce more ideas working in pairs.

Differentiation

For children who find it hard to get them started, use the grid for them to add their own ideas.

Creature	What does it do?
Worms	
Dogs	
Rabbits	
Humans	
Lions	
Spiders	
Roosters	
Donkeys	
Horses	

For children of lower ability, use the sheet on the next page, to get them started.

Plenary

Children read their poems, so far to the class. Encourage pupils to say what they like, or think is clever about each other's work.

Writing kennings is a suitable follow-up activity to writing list poems.

Link up with other subjects

As with any type of poem, it links up well with other curriculum areas because when they make their neat copy with the text in a column down the middle of the page, it leaves large areas for their own illustration. It can link up with ICT as children can type their poem and illustrate with pictures from the internet.

LIST POEMS

Fill in the blanks. Put in your own title. Add lines of you own if you can.

_____

Tadpoles jiggle

Worms _____

Wolves howl
Dogs _____

Lions hunt
Pigs _____

Larks sing
Monkeys _____

Eagles soar
Lions _____

Cats purr
Rabbits have _____

Whales blow
Roosters_____

Kittens play
Horses _____

Parrots squawk
Humans _____

Tigers pounce
Kangaroos _____

_____

_____

16   NARRATIVE POEMS

Narrative poems tell a story in an entertaining manner. They can be of any length, from a few verses to a whole book like the *Illiad*. They can be serious like *The Highwayman* by Alfred Noyes, or frivolous like *Jack and the Beanstalk* by Roald Dahl. There should be rhythm and most narrative poems have rhyme. The plot of the story need not be sophisticated. What matters is an entertaining choice of vocabulary. This is a challenging, but satisfying, activity for older Key Stage 2, and Key Stage 3 pupils. Depending on the class, the activities below should last for several lessons.

The picture book shelves in public libraries contain an entertaining selection of narrative tales in verse. Choose a few to use as examples.

Any story can be made into a narrative poem.

Lesson 1

Objective: to examine narrative poems, plan and begin writing a class narrative poem.

Warm-up

Read some narrative poems appropriate for the age group of the class and ask the children to tell you their reactions to them. Note what makes them interesting – they tell a story, rhythm, rhyme, vocabulary that is unusual and attention-grabbing, an ending which is satisfying or surprising.

Main part

For first attempts, it is sensible to choose a familiar story like *Cinderella, Little Red Riding Hood* or *The Three Little Pigs*. To plan the poem, divide the story into sections.

> The setting
>
> The characters
>
> The action – introduction
>
> > main action
> >
> > the ending

Invite the children to choose a story which everyone knows. Put the blank planning grid, shown below, onto the board or IWB for the class to fill in as a whole class activity. When they have filled in the middle column, ask them to think about rhyming words for the story. The second grid gives examples of the sorts of things they might suggest.

Setting		Rhyming words
Characters		
Plot	Beginning -	
	Main action –	
	End –	

Example

The Little Red Hen

		Rhyming words
Setting	A Farmyard	
Characters	The little red hen, the cat, the rat and the dog	rat, cat, sat hen, when
Plot	Beginning – The hen asks the others to help her to plant the wheat and they refuse so she plants it herself.	want , plant wheat, eat sun, anyone
	Main action – She asks them to help her to cut it, make flour and bake bread with it and each time they refuse so she does it herself.	cut, but no, go bake, take, make flour, hour do, you help, yelp
	End – The bread is ready to eat. They offer to help her to eat but she refuses and eats it herself.	farmyard, hard annoyed, enjoyed meet, eat

Emphasize the following points.

- Use a rhyming dictionary.

- Interesting vocabulary – similes, metaphors, onomatopoeia, alliteration, senses

- You do not have to describe the characters or setting at the beginning. That can be woven into the story. In fact, it is better to get straight into the action to grab the readers' attention, and slip the description into the action.

119

- Rhyming only works if the poem makes sense. It is better to get the story and rhythm going and then adjust for rhymes later, or leave them out if you cannot use suitable ones.

The children suggest lines to tell the story in verse. The hardest part is getting started so the teacher could suggest opening lines, like these for the Little Red Hen.

> One sunny day on the farmyard.
> The animals were resting in the sun.
> The little red hen said to her friends,
> 'Will you help me, anyone?

Write their suggestions on the board as they go along.

Plenary

Class reads the narrative poem so far. Ask children to comment on which parts sound well and which could be improved. Tell them that it will be finished in the next lesson.

Lesson 2

Objective: to complete the class narrative poem

Warm up

Recap on:-

> the characteristics of a narrative poem – tells a story, rhythm, rhyme;
>
> what makes it enjoyable – interesting vocabulary, similes, unusual rhymes, metaphors, onomatopoeia, senses, alliteration.

Main part

Children look at each section of their class notes and they jointly brainstorm ideas to complete the class narrative poem with everyone contributing. Either the teacher writes it on the board or an able writer scribes for the class.

Plenary

Class read the poem together and children comment on the parts which work well and suggest improvements for other parts.

Lesson 3

Objective: to plan a narrative poem in groups

Warm-up

Present the following lines orally, one at a time, for pupils to think up an interesting follow-on rhyming line for each.

> The piglets tired their mother pig out
>
> The fox went out hunting one day
>
> The cunning old wolf licked his jaws
>
> She rubbed and scrubbed and swept the floor
>
> The pussycats sang and danced in the moonlight

Main part

Ask children to suggest some well-known folk tales to use to write their own poem. Remind them of the characteristics of a narrative poem. Divide them into groups of three or four, ensuring that every group has a competent writer to scribe, or they can take turns to scribe. Each group discusses and decides which tale they want to use for their narrative poem and begins planning it collaboratively, writing their notes on a blank plan. When they have completed their sheet, collaboratively, they can begin composing their poem.

Differentiation

Children, who need support, work in a mixed ability group, or with the teacher in a support group. Use the story of The Three Billy Goats Gruff. Make sure everyone knows the story. Retell it if necessary and the children fill in the planning sheet. The teacher can use the notes in the grid to supplement the children's own ideas.

Setting	A riverbank with a bridge	Rhyming words
Characters	Little Billy Goat Gruff Medium Billy Goat Gruff Large Billy Goat Gruff Ugly troll	gruff, enough, stuff over, clover
Plot	Beginning – The goats want to cross the bridge over the river to get more sweet green grass. An ugly troll lives under the bridge.	long, strong sweet, eat, treat, feet scary, hairy scare, dare, beware
	Main action – in turn they try to cross the river. The troll wants to eat them. The first two tell him to eat the next troll and he lets them pass.	hasty, tasty woollie, bully shiver, river stared glared said, sped toward, roared
	End – The large Billy Goat Gruff tosses the troll into the river and they all get fat on the green grass.	Vicious, delicious Rushed, crushed Frowned drowned

Plenary

Children in each group read out their poem so far. Invite others to say which parts work well or make suggestions to improve it.

Lesson 4

Objective: to complete the narrative poems in groups

Warm-up

Pupils in their groups read their planning sheet.

Ask them to check that they have at least one example of onomatopoeia in their notes and give them a few minutes to put one in. Do the same with a simile, a metaphor, two examples of alliteration and at least three different senses. (You can omit any of these if the children are not familiar with them.)

Main part

In groups, children continue their narrative poems.

Differentiation

Pupils who need most support, can use the writing frame for the Three Billy Goats Gruff poem at the end of the chapter. They can use the words from their notes to fill in the blanks to complete their poem, working collaboratively in a group with a teacher to support, if necessary, or with their own sheets to write their own poem, depending on what they can manage. They can, of course, change any words on the sheet.

Some children find the hardest part is getting started. If necessary, they can use the first verse on the page to get going.

Plenary

Children enjoy an amusing ten minutes reading their poems, to their classmates. Encourage children to say what they like about each poem. (This a challenging activity so a further session may be needed to complete the poems.)

Link up with other subjects

Choose a story from your R.E. lessons and make notes to write it as a narrative poem.

Choose a story you have already written in a creative writing lesson and rewrite it as a poem.

Do not worry if you cannot get the rhyming perfect. Concentrate on getting the rhythm and interesting vocabulary right first.

THE THREE BILLY GOATS GRUFF

Three Billy Goats Gruff lay in their field
Munching the last of the grass and berries,
Eyeing the meadow across the river
With its trees of hazel nuts and cherries.

It had long _____

_____ as they looked over

The river _____

That speckled the meadow of daisies and clover.

The large billy goat had _____

His hair_____ long.

He had _____

His _____strong.

The middle-sized _____

With a _____ feet .

And the little _____

_____eat.

Under the bridge lived on the river _____

Lived _____scary.

He _____

The little billy _____wary.

Now continue the story. You can change the words at the beginning of the line if you want to. The rhyming words in bracket will help you to make it rhyme.

'Who's that _____

I'm hungry and_____

Don't eat me _____

Later_____

(eat meat sweet   hasty tasty   said sped instead)

Next the middle_____

_____

_____

_____

(decide eyed   woollie bully   toward roared   side stride)

The large _____

_____

_____

_____

(frowned drowned   rushed crushed   stare glare   shiver river

vicious delicious   shout stout)

17   NONSENSE RHYMES AND POEMS

This type of verse was made popular by Edward Lear. Children love nonsense rhymes and poems because of the humour and sheer stupidity of them. Many nursery rhymes contain at least an element of nonsense. The activities below are designed to span over a few lessons.

Lesson 1

Objective: to look at the characteristics of nonsense rhymes and write a whole class one

Warm up

Read the silly rhymes below.

Early one morning in the middle of the night
Two dead men got up and had a fight.   Traditional

In the month of Glasgow,
In the city of July,
The rain was snowing heavily
And the streets were warm and dry.
The roads were all deserted
With street parties in full swing.
There was perfect peace and quiet
And all were loudly singing.

The rhino is a pretty bird.
It leaps from grass to bough.
It builds its nest in a pasta tree
And whistles like a sow.   H.A.Bennett

THE OWL AND THE PUSSYCAT

The Owl and the Pussy-cat went to sea
In a beautiful pea green boat,
They took some honey, and plenty of money,
Wrapped up in a five pound note.
The Owl looked up to the stars above,

And sang to a small guitar,
'O lovely Pussy! O Pussy my love,
What a beautiful Pussy you are,
        You are,
        You are!
What a beautiful Pussy you are!'

Pussy said to the Owl, 'You elegant fowl!
How charmingly sweet you sing!
O let us be married! too long we have tarried:
But what shall we do for a ring?'
They sailed away, for a year and a day,
To the land where the Bong-tree grows
And there in a wood a Piggy-wig stood
With a ring at the end of his nose,
        His nose,
        His nose,
With a ring at the end of his nose.

'Dear pig, are you willing to sell for one shilling
Your ring?' Said the Piggy, 'I will.'
So they took it away, and were married next day
By the Turkey who lives on the hill.
They dined on mince, and slices of quince,
Which they ate with a runcible spoon;
And hand in hand, on the edge of the sand,
They danced by the light of the moon,
        The moon,
        The moon,
They danced by the light of the moon.   Edward Lear

Main part

Invite the children's comments and ask them to point everything which is stupid or plain

wrong. Ask them to tell you other characteristics of a nonsense poem. Check that they have

the following points.

- rhythm

- rhyme

- humour

- story (or description for shorter nonsense rhymes)

- made up words (Bong-tree)

- sheer impossibility of characters and events

Discuss what is nonsense in these and why.

Point out that the beauty of writing nonsense poems that they have everything absolutely under their control. They can make up words to rhyme and they can say anything they want, no matter how outrageous it may seem.

For two minutes, in pairs, children make up an opening nonsense line(s).

Invite children to tell their lines to the class. Choose one and write it on the board as the rhyme's opening line. If they are short of ideas, suggest these as opening lines.

One rainy day in the jungle…..

It was midnight in the classroom …..

The whale, the dolphin, the shark and the seal…..

The dinosaur called to his friends on the plain……

Ask them to suggest more lines to build up into a nonsense rhyme of four, six, or eight lines.

Plenary

Children read their class poem together. Challenge the children to think up humorous finishing off lines to the poem.

Lesson 2

Objective: to examine the features of narrative nonsense poems and write their own.

Warm up

For older key Stage 2 children read some of Edward Lear's wonderfully amusing nonsense poems. They can be googled easily. Below are popular nonsense poems which have stood the test of time.

The Jumblies

They went to sea in a sieve, they did,
In a sieve they went to sea:
In spite of all their friends could say,
On a winter's morn, on a stormy day,
In a sieve they went to sea!
And when the sieve turned round and round,

And every one cried, 'You'll all be drowned!'
They called aloud, 'Our sieve ain't big,
But we don't care a button! we don't care a fig!
In a sieve we'll go to sea!'
Far and few, far and few,
Are the lands where the Jumblies live;
Their heads are green, and their hands are blue,
And they went to sea in a sieve.

They sailed away in a sieve, they did,
In a sieve they sailed so fast,
With only a beautiful pea-green veil

Tied with a riband by way of a sail,
To a small tobacco-pipe mast;
And every one said, who saw them go,
'O won't they be soon upset, you know!
For the sky is dark, and the voyage is long,
And happen what may, it's extremely wrong
In a sieve to sail so fast!'
Far and few, far and few,
Are the lands where the Jumblies live;
Their heads are green, and their hands are blue,
And they went to sea in a sieve.

The water it soon came in, it did,
The water it soon came in;
So to keep them dry, they wrapped their feet
In a pinky paper all folded neat,
And they fastened it down with a pin.
And they passed the night in a crockery-jar,
And each of them said, 'How wise we are!
Though the sky be dark, and the voyage be long,
Yet we never can think we were rash or wrong,
While round in our sieve we spin!'
Far and few, far and few,
Are the lands where the Jumblies live;
Their heads are green, and their hands are blue,
And they went to sea in a sieve.

And all night long they sailed away;
And when the sun went down,
They whistled and warbled a moony song
To the echoing sound of a coppery gong,
In the shade of the mountains brown.
'O Timballo! How happy we are,
When we live in a sieve and a crockery-jar,

And all night long in the moonlight pale,
We sail away with a pea-green sail,
In the shade of the mountains brown!'
Far and few, far and few,
Are the lands where the Jumblies live;
Their heads are green, and their hands are blue,
And they went to sea in a sieve.

They sailed to the Western Sea, they did,
To a land all covered with trees,
And they bought an owl, and a useful cart,
And a pound of rice, and a cranberry tart,
And a hive of silvery bees.
And they bought a pig, and some green jack-daws,
And a lovely monkey with lollipop paws,
And forty bottles of Ring-bo-ree,
And no end of stilton cheese.
Far and few, far and few,
Are the lands where the Jumblies live;
Their heads are green, and their hands are blue,
And they went to sea in a sieve.

And in twenty years they all came back,
In twenty years or more,
And every one said, 'How tall they've grown!
For they've been to the Lakes, and the Torrible Zone,
And the hills of the Chankly Bore!'
And they drank their health, and gave them a feast
Of dumplings made of beautiful yeast;
And every one said, 'If we only live,
We too will go to sea in a sieve,
To the hills of the Chankly Bore!'
Far and few, far and few,
Are the lands where the Jumblies live;
Their heads are green, and their hands are blue,
And they went to sea in a sieve.   Edward Lear

THE BROOM, THE SHOVEL, THE POKER AND THE TONGS

The Broom and the Shovel, the Poker and Tongs,
They all took a drive in the Park;
And they each sang a song, ding-a-dong, ding-a-dong!
Before they went back in the dark.
Mr. Poker he sate quite upright in the coach;
Mr. Tongs made a clatter and clash;

Miss Shovel was dressed all in black (with a brooch);
Mrs. Broom was in blue (with a sash).
Ding-a-dong, ding-a-dong! And they all sang a song.
"O Shovely so lovely!" the Poker he sang,
"You have perfectly conquered my heart.
Ding-a-dong, ding-a-dong! If you're pleased with my song,
I will feed you with cold apple-tart.
When you scrape up the coals with a delicate sound,
Your nose is so shiny, your head is so round,
And your shape is so slender and bright!
Ding-a-dong, ding-a-dong! Ain't you pleased with my song?"
"Alas! Mrs. Broom," sighed the Tongs in his song,
"Oh! is it because I'm so thin,
And my legs are so long, ding-a-dong, ding-a-dong!
That you don't care about me a pin?
Ah! fairest of creatures, when sweeping the room,
Ah! why don't you heed my complaint?
Must you needs be so cruel, you beautiful Broom,
Because you are covered with paint?
Ding-a-dong, ding-a-dong! You are certainly wrong."
Mrs. Broom and Miss Shovel together they sang,
"What nonsense you're singing to-day!
"Said the Shovel, "I'll certainly hit you a bang!"
Said the Broom, "And I'll sweep you away!"
So the coachman drove homeward as fast as he could,
Perceiving their anger with pain;
But they put on the kettle, and little by little
They all became happy again.
Ding-a-dong, ding-a-dong!
There's an end of my song.   Edward Lear

Ask the children to give examples of these.

Words which show that these poems are old – coachman, riband, sash, shilling;

Onomatopoeia – ding-a-dong, clatter, clash

Made-up names – Jumblies, Torrible Zone, Shankly Bore, Ring-bo-ree, Timballo

Nonsense actions and situations

•   pinky paper to wrap up their feet
•   food items in verse 5

•   household objects being live people

- going to sea in a vessel made of holes
- appearance of the creatures
- tobacco pipe mast
- veil for a sail,
- crockery jar for shelter

Discuss the advantages of writing nonsense rhyme/story?

- You can use anything out of your imagination.

- You can put in foolish things like the food items in verse five of The Jumblies to make it rhyme.

- You can make up words like Torrible Bore and ring-bo-ree to make things rhyme.

- You can make it funny by making characters out of in everyday items like a brush and shovel

- The story is very simple.

To prepare to write their own nonsense poem, ask the class for ideas for these.
- a setting, real or imagined
- between two and four characters. They can be made up creatures, objects or creatures that already exist.
- a simple set of events to make a story, with satisfying ending.

Choose one of the children's ideas and, on the board, make a grid using the points above. Ask the children to brainstorm ideas to fill in each box in it. It might look like the grid on the next page.

Setting	Rain Forest
Characters	Sam, Eva and Ali - 3 children in an infant playground
Plot	Beginning - The kids find a play helicopter in the school playground and fly up and away.
	Middle – They fly over roof tops and over the sea and land in the Rain Forest. They meet lots of animals who play with them, give them rides, show them the rivers and tree tops. The children meet a panther and only just get into their helicopter in time.
	End – They fly over the forest, through the clouds and land safely in their playground.

Give each child a blank grid, or older children can copy it onto their books to fill in the details to write their own poem. Emphasize that they need not get the rhyme right at first. Concentrate on making it interesting and funny and getting the rhythm first. Children who find it difficult to think up and organize ideas can use the modelled plan above, or the class plan on the board.

Setting	
Characters	
Plot	Beginning -
	Main action –
	End –

Differentiation

For children who need learning support, this might be too challenging so they can use this verse from lesson 1 as their model. They may need to work with a teacher or teaching assistant.

> The rhino is a pretty bird.
> It flits from grass to bough.
> It builds its nest in a pasta tree
> And whistles like a sow.

Brainstorm lots of interesting words to help. Write their suggestions on the board. The following might help to enlarge their list.

> Movement words - waddles, skips, hops, jumps, leaps, flits, bounds, flies, trudges, glides, jogs, flaps,
> Creature sounds - hoots, whistles, chatters, bellows, thunders, roars, squeaks, cheeps, chirps, grunts, snorts, clucks, quacks, bleats, screams, yells, squawks.
> Creature homes - nest, sett, lair, den, hutch, burrow, warren.

Use the page at the end of the chapter page and give the children one or two verses each to fill in the blanks. Use their lists of words above to fill in the blanks to make their own nonsense verse. These lines on the next page are only suggestions. Of course the children can change any of the lines at the beginning or end. The rhyming words are already in place to allow the children to concentrate on rhythm and humorous vocabulary.

Plenary

Children read their poems so far. Encourage the children to suggest lines to follow what they have heard from their classmates and comment on which lines work well.

This is a challenging activity and will need further sessions to complete.

To link-up with other subjects

Use your ICT skills to find out some facts about the history of nonsense rhymes.

Find out the names of poets who have written nonsense poems in different centuries and read some of their poems to see how they have changed over the centuries and how they have stayed the same.

Write a funny nonsense rhyme about a day trip or a science experiment where everything goes wrong.

NONSENSE POEMS AND RHYMES

The _____ is a _____.

It _____ in the air.

It _____

And _____ like a bear.

The _____ is a _____.

It _____ up in trees.

It _____

And _____ like bees.

The _____ is a _____.

It _____ in the east.

It _____

And _____ like a wildebeast.

The _____ is a _____.

It _____ in the sea.

It _____

And _____ like a puppy.

The _____ is a _____.

It _____ in a _____ house.

It _____

And _____ like a mouse.

18   NURSERY RHYMES

Small children love nursery rhymes and it is a great opportunity for them to learn new vocabulary. Many originate from events in the past. Writing nursery rhymes gives children a chance to let their imagination to run riot. Key Stage 2 pupils find them easy to write because they can quite legitimately make them rhyme by using nonsense words and sentences. Take a well-known nursery rhyme and use it as a model.

Lesson 1

Objective: to write nursery rhymes using a familiar verse as a model

Warm up

Write this nursery rhyme on the board for the class to read. Tell them to think about the words, rhythm and rhyme.

Hey-diddle-diddle,
The cat and the fiddle.
The cow jumped over the moon.
The little dog laughed to see such fun
And the dish ran away with the spoon.

Ask the children to discuss the characteristics of the verse.

Check that they note

•   rhyme pattern a a b c b,

•   rhythm of each line,

•   fun, fantasy, nonsense.

•   Lines one and two are shorter than lines three, four and five.

•   Each line unrelated to the one before

Tell the children that it is easy to construct a similar type of nursery rhyme because you can invent words and phrases like 'Hey-diddle-diddle' and nonsense sentences to make it rhyme.

Main part

Give the children three minutes to talk to their partners to make up nonsense sentences. Ask for one sentence from each pair round the class. Write as many as you can manage on the board. It might look like this.

The dog played the piano.

The carrot fell out with the sausage.

The hamster threw the blackbird out.

The teddy bear fell over laughing.

The cucumber drank all the orange juice.

The monkey fell down the chimney.

The stars got fed up and went to bed.

The eagle played with the bluetit.

The chimney fell off the roof top.

The worm made the ladybird shout.

The fork danced with the carving knife.

The elephant danced in the moonlight.

The fox made friends with the chickens.

The pencils ran off with the writing pad.

The hens got a day off school.

Now point out the pattern to make their 'Hey-diddle-diddle' poems.

Line 1	A nonsense word to rhyme with line two (This should be done last.)
Line 2	A short line from the class list or one they have made up themselves
Line 3	The first of the two nonsense rhyming lines
Line 4	Another nonsense sentence
Line 5	The second rhyming nonsense line

Now plan the class rhyme. First, find two lines of which the two last words rhyme. If they cannot find two rhyming lines from the class list, then they can change one to create a rhyming line. Write their choice in lines three and five like this.

1

2

3   The monkey kicked over the stool.

4

5   The hens got a day off school.

Add another silly sentence to line 4. Tell them this is easy because it does not have to rhyme.

1

2

3   The monkey kicked over the stool

4   The teddy bear fell over laughing

5   And the hens got a day off school

Now think of a short second line and make up a short nonsense word to rhyme with it. They might suggest something like this.

1   Bananarano.

2   The dog played piano.

3   The monkey kicked over the stool.

4   The teddy bear fell over laughing

5   And the hens got a day off school.

Let the children read it together to give them a sense of achievement. Pupils write their own nursery rhyme, following this model.

Differentiation

The next page can be used by children who need support.

Plenary

Either pupils read their nursery rhymes to the rest of the class or, give the children these lines to start and five minutes, in pairs, to think up finishing lines and read them to the class. Emphasise that only the 3rd and 5th line need to rhyme.

    Too woo, too whit.
    The fox and the bluetit.

NURSERY RHYMES

Use these to fill in the blanks to make you own 'Hey-diddle-diddle' nursery rhymes. You can change any of the words if you want to.

_____

The spoon _____.

The bear_____ cricket bat.

The wolf sang_____

And the octopus _____ hat.

_____

The snake _____.

The trees _____ sun.

The pussy cat _____

_____fun.

_____

The cuckoo _____

The toy soldier _____ drum.

The Sindy doll _____

_____ his mum.

Lesson 2

Objective: to write a nursery rhyme, using a familiar rhyme as a model.

Warm –up

Read this nursery rhyme and ask the children to tell you its characteristics.

Georgie Porgie, pudding and pie
Kissed the girls and made them cry.
When the boys came out to play
Georgie Porgie ran away.

Make sure they have noted the following points.

- rhyme scheme a a b b

- rhythm - 4 beats (feet) per line

- The first line starts with a name and rhyming nonsense word, and something unrelated.

Point out the pattern for writing a rhyme in this model.

Line 1   the name of the person with a rhyming nonsense word, unrelated to the name. (This can be written second to make it rhyme with the next line of the poem.)

Line 2   action (Write this one first.)

Lines 3 and 4   a reaction in a rhyming couplet (These are written last.)

Give pupils, in pairs, two minutes to write down children's actions which might cause a reaction. Ask each pair to read one out to the class and write as many as you can on the board. It might look like this.

batted the ball through a window

threw his dinner on the floor

never did his homework

made a mess in her bedroom

pushed a child off a swing

ran away from his mum

kicked a policemen in the shins

pushed an old man into the holly bush

stole the cakes from the baker's shop

let the vicar's tyres down

knocked people's doors and ran away

wrote horrid graffiti on garden walls

Main part

Now plan the poem. Choose one to use as line 2 and write it on the board following the plan below.

1

2   Let the vicar's tyres down

3

4

Now ask the children for a name, a rhyming sound and anything (sense or nonsense) that rhymes with 'down'. Add it to line one.

Example

1   Lennie Penny lives in town

2   Let the vicar's tyres down.

3

4

Now ask the children to suggest reactions to Lenny's behaviour.

Examples The vicar grabbed him and made him pump them up again.

      He had to sweep the floor of the church out every day for a week.

      He had to spend hours cutting the grass in the churchyard.

      His parents were furious and gave him a nasty punishment

Ask pupils to suggest words which will make a rhyming couplet.

      Sweep, weep   hard, churchyard   roar, floor   mean, clean   pain, again

Pupils use them to make a rhyming couplet.

Examples   The punishment had him weeping
            In the church, dusting and sweeping.

            Lennie though it very hard.
            He had to weed the whole churchyard.

            Lennie began to howl and roar
            When he had to sweep the whole church floor.

            His parents thought him very mean
            And made him make the whole church clean.

            Lenny's arms ached with pain
            When he had to pump them up again.

Now put it all together.

            Lennie Pennie lives in town,
            Let the vicar's tyres down.
            His parents thought his very mean
            And made him make the whole church clean.

Tell children that it is important that the last word in line 2 has got lots of rhyming pairs, so

words like 'window' need to be changed to 'window pane'.

Example

1
2   Batted her ball through a window pane.
3
4

Now think of a name and a rhyme, and something to rhyme with 'pane'.

1   Rosie Posy, showers of rain
2   Batted the ball through a window pane.

Ask the children to think of a reaction.

Examples   She had to sweep up the glass.

            She had to pay for a new pane.

            She ran away and blamed it on someone else.

            He parents took her bat and ball away

143

Now think up rhyming pairs

Pane, again   glass, crass   blame, shame   away, day, say

Use these to make up a couplet to finish the rhyme.

> The owner thought this very crass
> And made her pay for a pane of glass.

Now put it all together.

1	Rosie Posy, showers of rain
2	Batted the ball through a window pane.
3	The owner thought this very crass
4	And made her pay for a pane of glass.

Pupils can work in pairs, or singly, to make their own notes and use them and the notes suggested by the class to write their own `Georgie Porgie´ nursery rhyme.

Differentiation

Children who need support, can use the skeleton plan at the end of the chapter.

Plenary

Pupils read their poems to the class. Encourage the pupils to say what they like about them.

To link up with other subjects

Surf the net to find the origin of these nursery rhymes and any others which you like.

Baa-baa black sheep,

Ring-a-ring of roses,

Pop goes the weasel,

London Bridge is falling down,

Mary, Mary quite contrary.

NURSERY RHYMES

Fill in the blanks to make a Georgie Porgie style nursery rhyme. You can use the rhyming words at the end of each rhyme or change any of the words on the lines.

_____

Broke a computer in the suite.

The teacher _____

_____

ended, suspended   rain, again   play, away

_____

Threw stones at a tiger in the zoo.

The zoo keeper _____

_____

displeased, seized   rage, cage   grim, him   annoy, boy

_____

Threw snowballs at his nursery teacher

The children _____

_____

snow, woe, go   choking, soaking   fright, snow fight, white,

horrified, cried, hide, outside, slide

19   SHAPE POEMS

A shape poem is one in which the words are written in the shape of the subject of the poem. It can be descriptive or narrative. Shape poems do not have to rhyme but, of course, it is more impressive if they do.

Perhaps the most famous one is Mouse's sad tale in Alice in Wonderland. Alice imagines that he is telling about his tail and so the poem is written in the shape of a mouse's tail.

Lesson 1
Objective: to understand the format of a shape poem and write a class shape poem

Warm up
Read Lewis Carroll's shape poem and the other examples of shape poems below and invite the children's comments.

Children must see the poems, so they can be photocopied or scanned onto an IWB.

The Mouse's Tale from 'Alice in Wonderland'.

'Fury said to a
mouse, That he
met in the
house,
"Let us
both go to
law: I will
prosecute
you. Come,
I'll take no
denial; We
must have a
trial; For
really this
morning I've
nothing to do."
Said the
mouse to the
cur, "Such
a trial,
dear Sir,
With
no jury
or judge
would be
wasting
our breath,"
'I'll be
judge, I'll
be jury,"
Said
cunning
Old Fury:
'I'll try
the whole
cause,
and
condemn
you
to
death." '

Lewis Carroll

147

Snake

Slipping
    and slithering
        slowly through grasses. Silently spying as everything passes.
                Not a sound from him is heard. Until he
                                      pounces
                                  on a
                                little
                              bird.

Football

A perfect sphere.
Every boy loves to feel
those strips of leather, stit-
ched together. Full of air, yet
hard as steel. Loved by all, yet
kicked everywhere. It soars
high into the air and then
everyone dashes to it.

Story book

Wood processed into thin, thin leaves.
Carefully trimmed to a perfect stack
covered in dots and squiggles in black,
in parallel rows like railway tracks.
A performing magician when it's read,
for creating pictures in my head.

                                         H. A. Bennett

Make sure the children have noted the following.

- the shape reflects the topic

- descriptive language

- metaphor (a performing magician)

- similes

- rhyming words go anywhere, not necessarily the end of the line

- rhythm

- alliteration

- the lines do not have to begin with a capital

- strong verbs (spying, creating, dashes).

Point out that shape poems must be in the shape of the title, and the other points improve the poem.

Main part

Ask children to tell you, in one or two words, something they love.

Choose one subject and start modelling the notes on the board using these as prompts

- Descriptive phrases (sight, sound, smell, taste, feel)

- What it does

- What it is used for

- How it makes you feel

The notes might look like this.

Mango

tropical   juicy   delicious   tangy   smooth skinned

green and red merging into each other   fibrous flesh

hard stone surrounded by the flesh   quenches a thirst   satisfies

super in fruit salad

Invite children's suggestions to write sentences and phrases about mangoes and write them on your board or type onto an IWB. Tell them to concentrate on interesting, descriptive vocabulary. They might suggest something like this.

> Mangoes have smooth green and red skin.
> It tastes delicious.
> I love to bite into it and suck out the flavour.
> It has soft, juicy fibres round a hard stone.
> It quenches my thirst.

Teaching points

Whatever topic the class chooses, you can use points like these to help make it more powerful.

- Explain that rhymes are not essential, but it is better to have some.

- Change words to make rhymes, as long as they are suitable words. They can be anywhere in the verse.

  Example - green and red skin, keeping delicious flavours in

149

- You can make it more powerful by cutting out words like 'It has' and starting the sentence with the interesting words.

  Example – change 'It has soft juicy fibres round a hard stone'

  to 'Soft juicy fibres round a hard stone'.

- Improve it by adding a simile. Look at your adjectives and try to put one in.

  Example, 'a hard stone' sounds better as 'a stone as hard as steel'.

- Improve it further. Strong verbs paint a better picture.

  Example,   'soft juicy fibres round a hard stone'

  sounds better as 'soft juicy fibres cling to a hard stone'.

- Sometimes you can leave out words like 'and'.

  Example – 'green, red skin' sounds better than 'green and red skin'

- Alliteration grabs people's attention.

  Example – 'a delicious taste' is better as 'a tangy taste'

Draw a large mango (or other) shape on the board and start filling in the improved version. It might look something like this.

> Smooth, strong
> green red skin, keeping delicious
> flavours in. Peal it with a knife blade
> to reveal hundreds of juicy fibres clinging
> to a stone as hard as steel. My teeth sink in.
> They love to taste the tangy flesh. It sends
> a ripple along my tongue. My thirst
> has gone away.

Plenary

Read the class poem and invite children to say what they think is best about it. Remind them of the meaning of metaphor and ask children to offer suggestions on how it could be improved further, by adding a metaphor.

Tell the children that in their next lesson they will write their own shape poem. Pets are a good subject because children who have a pet, usually have an emotional reaction to it. Those who do not have a pet can choose a creature which they particularly like. Give pupils two minutes silent thinking time to decide the subject of their own shape poem.

Lesson 2

Objective: to write own shape poem

Warm up

Recap on the characteristics of a shape poem. If you have an IWB this website,

http://www.primaryresources.co.uk/english/docs/shape_poems.doc and others show a

few examples.

Main part

Children then follow the pattern of the previous lesson to write their notes for their own

shape poem. Write down their title and add their notes and compose their poem.

Write these words on your board to keep them at the front of the children's minds.

- Descriptive phrases (sight, sound, smell, taste, feel)

- What it does

- How it makes you feel

Improve your style

Use any three of these.

- alliteration

- rhyme

- rhythm

- simile

- strong verb

When children are satisfied with their shape poem, they can draw or trace or a picture of

their pet or draw round a template on white paper. Clip their white sheet on top of the line-

guide so that the children can write inside the shape in neat lines.

Differentiation

For children who need support, use the sheets on the next pages to get them started.

Extension

Write a shape poem which contains at least four of these - an alliteration, a simile, a strong

verb, a metaphor, onomatopoeia, rhythm and some rhyming.

Plenary

Children read out their poems to the class without a title for classmates to guess the type of animal. Invite children to say what they like about their classmates poems.

Link-up with other subjects

Choose a leader they are studying in history or RE and make a suitable outline on a page. For example, if it is a monarch, an outline of a large crown. For Boudicca, a chariot. For a Greek or Roman leader, an outline of a human shape in a toga or appropriate dress. Write your shape poem to insert into the outline.

Whatever country they are studying in geography, make an outline of the map of the country to write their poem inside.

Make an outline of a piece of scientific equipment like a test tube, a Bunsen burner, a bulb, battery or a magnet and write a few descriptive sentences inside.

SHAPE POEMS

Put in the name of your pet and add some words and phrases of your own to the ones below.

_____ (Cat's name)

Describe your cat sight sound touch smell	a bundle of fluff cuddly
How does it make you feel?	makes me feel loved
What does it do?	hunts at night pads along quietly sleeps in her basket
Alliteration	smooth soft fur
Simile	pounces like a tiger
strong verb	Springs

Use the phrases above to write some sentences for your poem. Try to put in a pair of rhyming words.

_____

_____

_____

_____

_____

Put in the name of your pet or other creature and add some words and phrases of your own to the ones below.

_____ (Dog's name)

Describe your dog sight sound touch smell	shaggy coat
How does it make you feel?	happy that he is my friend
What does it do?	begs for biscuits licks me
Alliteration	jumps for joy
Simile	runs like the wind
strong verb	rushes to meet me

Use the phrases above to write some sentences for your poem. Try to put in a pair of rhyming words.

_____

_____

_____

_____

_____

Books by Hazel Bennett

Continuum International   2nd Edition 2009   ISBN 978 1 84706 056 3

First published in April 2006

Teacher training has a high drop-out rate and this does not help a profession which has a shortage of members in some areas. This manual aims to guide student teachers and encourage them to keep going, through their college work and teaching practices and finding their first job.

It is written sensitively to reassure students that they can rise above the difficulties and go on confidently to be successful teachers.

'The Trainee Teachers' Survival Guide' covers just about everything someone contemplating or undertaking a PGCE course could want to know... The sections on reflective practice, parents' evenings and balancing teaching with a family are particularly useful.'

Sarah Bubb, Times educational Supplement.   First Edition

The NQTeachers' Survival Guide
How to pass your induction year with flying colours

Edgware Books   **ISBN** 978 0 9574648 3 4   Also available on Kindle

For both Primary and Secondary teachers, **The NQTeachers' Survival Guide** is a step-by-step manual, on how to face the induction year which, for many teachers can be the most challenging of their career. It aims to smooth teachers' paths through a daunting list of tasks so that they persevere until the end of the year, pass with flying colours and confidently go on to enjoy satisfying and successful careers.

It is written in a jargon-free language and packed with practical tips on how to cope with every issue from starting off on the right foot to establish constructive relationships with pupils, colleagues, non-teaching staff, the head and parents, right through each step to the end of the year.

Class Assemblies for Primary Schools

Published in April 2007 by Educational
Printing Services ISBN 1 905637 14 4
Includes the right for the
owner to photocopy.

Available at enquires@eprint.co.uk
Tel (01254) 882080,

This wide-ranging and practical book includes a chapter on tips for presenting successful assemblies, followed by 36 delightful scripts, for Key Stage 2 classes to perform.

The scripts cover all the main world religions, Black History and 10 secular scripts from Boudicca to Mother Teresa. Written in a mixture of prose and humorous rhyme-and-mime verse, each playlet is designed to involve every member of the class in the speech and action.

'A whole year's worth of weekly assemblies catering for our multicultural society, all in witty, highly original rhyme, with plenty of production tips. Sparkling with good humour, informative and fun – this is a real gift for hard-pressed teachers . . .'

Kate Nivison   'Women Writers' Network News'.

'Superb scripts in which every child plays a valued role. The rhyming aspect motivates and excites the children, enhancing the confidence and esteem of all, resulting in an excellent performance.'

Rochelle Waghorn, class teacher, who has successfully used some of them.

'Hazel Bennett has produced a life saver…' Henry Phillips   Prep School

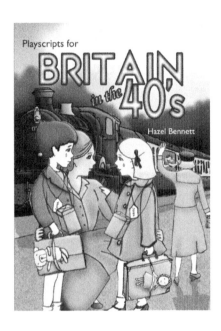

Playscripts for Britain in the 40s

This book of four play scripts is ideal for pupils in Key Stage 2, who are studying World War II and beyond. It explores the experience of war through the eyes of the people involved. Each story has a plot to engage the children's interest as they see how everyone coped with the hardships and upheavals and rose above them.

Children, who are reluctant to read on their own, can enjoy reading the stories in a social group, while gaining an understanding of life in war-time Britain.

Educational Printing Services
ISBN 987 1 905637 41 6
Order online RRP £5.99 Available at www.eprint.co.uk
Tel 01254 882080
Fax 01254 882010

CPSIA information can be obtained at www.ICGtesting.com
Printed in the USA
LVOW02s1534170314

377755LV00015B/922/P